# Maltipoo Complete Owner's Manual.

# Maltipoo facts and information.

# Maltipoo care, costs, feeding, health and training all included.

## by

## Elliott Lang

# Maltipoo Owner's Manual.

# Table of Contents

Table of Contents.................................................................3

Foreword..........................................................................9

**Chapter 1) Breed Basics** ................................................**10**

    *1) Breed Qualities*................................................. 10

    *2) Temperament*.................................................. 12

    *3) Breed Standard* ............................................... 12

    *4) Hypoallergenic Qualities* .................................. 13

    *5) Maltipoos as Purse Dogs*.................................. 14

    *6) Veterinary Care* .............................................. 16

    *7) Insurance*....................................................... 17

    *8) Yearly Costs* ................................................... 17

    *9) Myths* ........................................................... 18

    *10) Trainability* .................................................. 19

    *11) Summing Up: Pros and Cons* ........................... 20

**Chapter 2) The Maltipoo as a Pet**................................**21**

    *1) Price* ............................................................. 22

    *2) Internet Puppy Scam* ...................................... 23

    *3) A Word About Pet Shops* .................................. 24

    *4) Finding a Breeder*........................................... 25

    *5) Showing* ........................................................ 28

    *6) The Myth of Hybrid Vigor* ................................ 28

    *7) Rescues*......................................................... 29

    *8) Should I Have a Maltipoo?*................................ 30

## Table of Contents

9) Pet Insurance ........................................................................ 34

10) Maltipoos and Other Dogs ................................................ 34

11) Maltipoos and Cats .......................................................... 35

12) Maltipoos as Therapy Animals and Companions ................ 36

13) Licensing ......................................................................... 36

14) When to Bring Your Puppy Home ..................................... 37

15) Who Shouldn't Have a Maltipoo? ...................................... 37

**Chapter 3) Bringing Home a Maltipoo Puppy ...........................38**

1) Puppy-Proofing the House ................................................. 38

2) Finding Pet Services ......................................................... 42

3) Talking to Your Children ................................................... 43

4) Preparing Other Pets ........................................................ 44

5) Getting a Puppy Room ...................................................... 44

6) Should I Get More Than One? ............................................ 45

7) Boy or Girl? ...................................................................... 45

8) Common Mistakes to Avoid ............................................... 46
   a) Sleeping in Your Bed ..................................................... 46
   b) Picking Them Up at the Wrong Time .............................. 46
   c) Playing Too Hard or Too Long ....................................... 46
   d) Hand Play .................................................................... 47
   e) Distraction and Replacement ........................................ 47

9) The First Weeks With Your Puppy ...................................... 48
   a) The First Night ............................................................. 48
   b) The First Week ............................................................. 51

**Chapter 4) Supply Basics .......................................................54**

1) Bed .................................................................................. 54

2) Bowls ............................................................................... 54

3) Collar/Harness ................................................................. 54

4) Leash ............................................................................... 55

# Table of Contents

5) Puppy Food ............................................................................ 55

6) Toys .................................................................................... 56

7) Puppy Pads ........................................................................... 56

8) Baggies/Baggie Dispensers .................................................... 57

9) Grooming Supplies ................................................................ 57

10) Toothbrush/Toothpaste ...................................................... 57

11) Dog Carrier ........................................................................ 58

12) Towels .............................................................................. 58

**Chapter 5) Maltipoo Care** ....................................................... **60**

1) Feeding ............................................................................... 60

2) Exercise .............................................................................. 61

3) Weather .............................................................................. 62

4) Teething ............................................................................. 63

5) Neutering and Spaying .......................................................... 64
   a) What is Neutering? ............................................................ 65
   b) Neutering Males ................................................................ 65
   c) What is Spaying? ............................................................... 66
   d) Effects on Aggression ........................................................ 66
   e) Spaying Females ............................................................... 67
   f) Effects on General Temperament ......................................... 67
   g) Effects on Escape and Roaming .......................................... 68
   h) Effects on Problem Elimination .......................................... 68
   i) Possible Weight Gain ......................................................... 69

6) Caring for a Rescue Maltipoo ................................................. 69

**Chapter 6) Maltipoo Grooming** ................................................ **73**

1) The Basics ........................................................................... 75

2) Bathing ............................................................................... 76

3) Professional Grooming .......................................................... 78

4) Clipping .............................................................................. 80

5) Nail Care ............................................................................. 80

*6) Maltipoo Fur Type* ........................................................................... *83*

*7) Ear Care* ............................................................................................ *84*

*8) Eye Care* ........................................................................................... *85*

*9) Dental Care* ...................................................................................... *85*

*10) Skin Care* ........................................................................................ *91*

*11) Brushing and Combing* .................................................................. *91*

*12) Bleaching* ....................................................................................... *92*

*13) Equipment & Supplies Required* .................................................. *93*

*14) The Older Maltipoo* ....................................................................... *95*

*15) Grooming Products* ....................................................................... *96*
    a) Shampoos ................................................................................. 96
    b) Conditioners ............................................................................. 97
    c) De-tanglers ............................................................................... 97
    d) Styptic Powder ......................................................................... 98
    e) Ear Powders .............................................................................. 99
    f) Ear Cleaning Solutions .............................................................. 99
    g) Home Ear Cleaning Solutions .................................................. 99
    h) Canine Toothpastes ............................................................... 100
    i) Paw Creams ............................................................................ 101

**Chapter 7) Training a Maltipoo** .......................................................**102**

*1) House Training* .............................................................................. *102*
    a) Human Training ...................................................................... 102
    b) Bell Training ........................................................................... 105
    c) Kennel Training ...................................................................... 106
    d) Exercise Pen Training ............................................................. 107
    e) Puppy Apartment™ Training ................................................. 108
    f) Free Training .......................................................................... 110
    g) Professional Cleaning Products ............................................. 111

*2) Barking* .......................................................................................... *112*

*3) Play Biting* ..................................................................................... *114*

*4) Begging* .......................................................................................... *115*

*5) Sit* ................................................................................................... *115*

*6) Come* .............................................................................................. *116*

# Table of Contents

7) Heel............................................................................................ 116

8) Separation Anxiety ................................................................. 118

9) Socialization and Bonding ..................................................... 120

10) Tips for Training Your Maltipoo........................................... 123

11) Treats or Not? ........................................................................ 125

   a) Treats to Avoid............................................................... 126

   b) Healthy Treats ............................................................... 127

12) Escapes.................................................................................... 129

**Chapter 8) Maltipoo Health** ...................................................**130**

1) Tear staining............................................................................ 131

2) Anal Gland Issues ................................................................... 132

3) Pattellar Luxation ................................................................... 133

4) Legg-Calvé-Perthes Disease .................................................. 135

5) White Dog Shaking Syndrome................................................ 136

6) Tracheal Collapse ................................................................... 137

7) Hypoglycemia........................................................................... 138

8) Heat Stress ............................................................................... 140

9) Poisoning.................................................................................. 142

10) Choking .................................................................................. 143

**Chapter 9) A Quick Word About Breeding**.............................**145**

**Chapter 10) Poisonous Foods & Plants**..................................**148**

1. Poisonous Foods ..................................................................... 148

2. Poisonous Household Plants................................................... 154

3. Poison Proof Your Home ........................................................ 160

4. Garden Plants.......................................................................... 160

5. Grass ........................................................................................ 161

6. Animal Poison Control Centre............................................... 161

# Table of Contents

**Chapter 11) Caring for Aging Dogs** ............................................................ **162**

*1. What to Be Aware Of* ............................................................ *162*
    a) Physiological Changes ............................................ 162
    b) Behavioral Changes ................................................ 162
    c) Geriatric Dogs ....................................................... 163
    d) More Bathroom Breaks .......................................... 164

*2. How to Make Them Comfortable* .......................................... *165*
    a) Regular Checkups ................................................... 165
    b) No Rough Play ........................................................ 165
    c) Mild Exercise .......................................................... 165
    d) Best Quality Food ................................................... 166
    e) Clean and Parasite Free .......................................... 166
    f) Plenty of Water ....................................................... 166
    g) Keeping Warm ....................................................... 167
    h) Indoor Clothing ..................................................... 167
    i) Steps or Stairs ........................................................ 167
    j) Comfortable Bed .................................................... 168
    k) More Love and Attention ....................................... 168

*3. What is Euthanasia?* ............................................................ *168*

*4. When to Help a Dog Transition* ............................................ *169*

*5. Grieving a Lost Pet* ............................................................. *171*

*6. The Rainbow Bridge Poem* ................................................... *173*

*7. Memorials* ......................................................................... *174*

**Maltipoo Resources** ............................................................... **175**

*1) Information* ....................................................................... *175*

*2) Breeders* ........................................................................... *175*

*4) Equipment* ........................................................................ *175*

**Index** .................................................................................. **177**

# Foreword

When you have decided to bring a dog into your life, there are many different options open to you. Choosing the right dog is a process that takes time and effort, but in the end you are rewarded with a companion animal that suits your home and your family.

The maltipoo is a relatively new hybrid dog breed, and though they are quite popular, there are a few unknowns that must be considered. On the other hand, they are lively, energetic dogs that can do wonderfully in a wide variety of settings.

Whether you are looking for dogs that do well for families or you are looking for a companion animal for yourself, there are many reasons to be drawn to the maltipoo.

Learn more about this breed and what it might be like to have a maltipoo in your home and sharing your life.

# Chapter 1) Breed Basics

## 1) Breed Qualities

The maltipoo, also known as the maltepoo, and the maltapoo, is a dog that is produced from a Maltese poodle mix. As you look up miniature Maltese dogs and teacup Maltese dogs for sale, you will see more and more ads for maltipoos for sale, and you might find yourself wondering what this breed is like.

Maltipoo, Maltapoo, Multipoo, Malte-Poo, Multa-Poo, Maltepoo are all different spellings for the same dog.

The maltipoo was bred to be a superb companion animal, and this is reflected in its size. The question of how big maltipoos are is common, and there is actually some variance. As an adult, the maltipoo stands between 8 and 14 inches high or 20 and 35 centimeters, with the taller examples of the breed coming from miniature poodle parentage rather than from toy poodle (also known as teacup poodles) parentage.

How tall they become and how much they weigh is difficult to say as that usually depends on the Poodle but to give you an idea: their weight is usually between 5 and 12 pounds or 2,5kg and 6 kg.

They remain rather fragile dogs for their entire lives. Their small size can make them accident prone in a busy house, especially as they are highly curious dogs that love to see what you are doing.

Although some sites claim that the maltipoo can live to be 16-years-old or more, it is generally accepted that maltipoos typically live between 10 and 13 years.

There is no breed standard for the maltipoo, and although there are several organizations that have them registered and recognized as a breed, there is little consensus regarding what this dog should look like or whether there is any breed conformation that it should follow.

One variation of this dog looks a great deal like a Maltese with slightly wavy or kinky hair, other variations are larger with coats that look rather rough.

The most common color for maltipoos is white, as Malteses are always white. However, poodles come in a wide variety of colors, including blue, silver and cream, and crossbreeding results in some of these colors transferring over to the offspring. Maltipoos that have markings of any sort are a little more rare, as only poodles have markings themselves.

Although white is the most common color, you are just as likely to find a black maltipoo, a red maltipoo, or an apricot maltipoo in the litters you are looking at. Although a white maltipoo is iconic, perhaps one of these other breed colors will win your heart!

Maltipoos tend to have short faces and rather stubby legs, and their tails are comparatively short as well.

Because of the fact that most maltipoos descend from two purebred dogs of different lineages, it is hard to pinpoint what health problems they might inherit. It is generally safe to assume that if you choose a maltipoo, you should keep an eye out for any problems that affect poodles and Malteses.

Remember as you search for your perfect dog that there is no such thing as a teacup maltipoo. There is no standardization for this term, and no clear meaning assigned to it regarding the dog's size. While looking up things like teacup chihuahua puppies, toy Maltese dogs and miniature Maltese for sale can give you results, looking up teacup maltipoo puppies for sale will tend to get you some rather questionable breeders.

It is worth noting that they are typically quite high in energy, and that this is not something that really goes away as they get older. These dogs are often known to act like puppies for their entire lives, with lively natures that mean that they want to play a lot!

## 2) Temperament

When it comes to character, maltipoo dogs are very sweet. They tend to be fairly high in energy, and they are quite intelligent on top of this.

All of this put together can make for a dog that is a little challenging if you have never cared for a puppy before. The energy of this breed should not be underestimated, and that means that you should be willing and able to keep up with it.

The intelligence of the maltipoo dog is a plus when you want an animal that understands its obedience lessons, but it also means that your dog can have a mind of its own on certain things. The high intelligence also means that your dog can get quite bored very easily, and when it comes to destruction, there is nothing quite as creative as a bored, intelligent dog!

Your dog's temperament should be a selling point, and if you want a smart, energetic dog, you want a maltipoo. If you are worried about giving your dog enough time and exercise, or if you are worried that you are not going to be able to train it, you may need a different breed or even a different pet.

As with any other dog, the best way to be sure of the animal's temperament is to make sure that you treat it right from the very beginning. A puppy is a blank slate, and though it will certainly have its own personality, you can make sure that it receives all of its training.

## 3) Breed Standard

Although the maltipoo is not a breed that is recognized by the American Kennel Club, there are many people who consider it to be a legitimate breed. For example, the North American Maltipoo Club and Registry offers some strict guidelines on which dogs can and should be considered a maltipoo.

At the most basic level, a maltipoo is a Maltese/poodle cross. The poodle must be classified as a toy poodle or a miniature poodle, and no other dog breeds may be involved in the process.

One acceptable example of maltipoo genetics involves a purebred poodle and a purebred Maltese. A second acceptable example of maltipoo genetics includes the breeding of two maltipoos together. Adding another breed to the mix creates a mixed-breed dog that cannot be called a maltipoo.

When you are looking into finding the right breeder from which to purchase a companion, make sure that you consider what they define as a maltipoo and what you need to know.

It is not snobbery to insist upon a certain genetic background for your maltipoo. Instead, it is simply doing your research to make sure that you are getting what you pay for. A maltipoo is very much a new breed of dog, and unlike breeds like the golden retriever or the beagle, there is a lot of dissent on what makes a "real" maltipoo.

Educate yourself and make sure that you understand what you are getting in to.

## 4) Hypoallergenic Qualities

One reason why people are drawn to maltipoos is that they are considered to be hypoallergenic dogs. Before you invest in a maltipoo for this reason, there are a few things to keep in mind.

Firstly, there is no such thing as a dog that is completely hypoallergenic. If you are allergic to dogs, you are allergic to the dander that falls off of the dog's skin. There is no dog that does not create dander. Instead, there are dogs that simply shed dander much less than other dogs do.

Maltipoos are bred from the Maltese and the poodle. Both of these breeds are highly recommended for people who are sensitive to animal dander. If your allergy is mild or even moderate, there is a chance that you will not have a problem with these dogs.

If you purchase a maltipoo, you can generally expect these hypoallergenic qualities to be passed on to your dog. However, there are a few things to keep in mind.

Firstly, you must consider how allergic you really are. Make sure that you spend some time with maltipoos in general. Do your eyes water and do you have any rashes after playing with the dogs? In some cases, these symptoms will go away after you have exposed yourself to one specific dog for a long enough interval. If you are having serious issues with maltipoos from the beginning, however, it might be time to consider another pet.

Another thing to remember is that there are a lot of dogs out there that are sold as maltipoos but have some unclear ancestry in their background. Remember that a real maltipoo only has poodle and Maltese blood. A puppy that is sold as a maltipoo but has cocker spaniel or golden retriever blood in its veins may well have inherited some more triggering dander as well!

If you are in a spot to consider getting a dog for hypoallergenic purposes, be willing to spend some time choosing the right dog for you. Maltipoos are crossbreeds, and at this point, the breed is new enough that it is impossible to say anything precise about the breed as a whole.

There's nothing quite as heartbreaking as bringing a puppy home only to find out that you cannot keep it, so make sure that you know what your allergy tolerance is before you step forward to choose this breed.

## 5) Maltipoos as Purse Dogs

Over the past fifteen years or so, there has been a trend for people to carry very small dogs in their purses when they go out and about. There are a number of breeds that are used for this purpose, including the teacup maltese, the teacup poodle, and dogs that are known as Maltese toy dogs. Maltipoos, because of their diminutive size, seem like a good candidate for this treatment, but the truth is that carrying a dog in a purse is always a bad idea.

People who are fans of purse dogs argue that this is a simple thing that does not harm the dog. It gives the dog a chance to see the city from the safety of a certain height, and it helps the dog get from place to place.

While it is true that some people use purses designed for carrying dogs as dog carriers, the truth is that a real dog carrier made from nylon stretched over a solid frame or hard plastic is a far better choice. When you are taking a dog from place to place, the last thing that you want is for it to be able to jump out of your purse. Some of these purses do have leash and collar attachments, but these devices have a much higher chance of choking your dog than keeping it where you want it.

If you need to take your dog from place to place, and when you are worried about it being trampled underfoot, a solid carrier is a much better choice.

Another reason to avoid putting your maltipoo into a purse is that it will make it uncomfortable. Maltipoos are dogs that are bred to be companions, and while it is certainly true that they love to be with you at all times, they do not love to be carried in a swaying bag several feet off of the ground.

When you are cuddling your maltipoo at home, chances are good that you are carrying it close to your body with your arms supporting it. You will also likely be sitting with it in your lap or letting it sprawl on your chest or belly.

When you are carrying a maltipoo around in a purse, you will find that it feels a lot more unstable, and this in turn leads to a lot of bad behavior and a lot of stress.

Maltipoos are dogs that do not handle stress very well. They are known for being lively and active, but they are not comfortable when they are put into situations where they are very uncomfortable.

With that in mind, the maltipoo is a breed that does not like to have a lot of swaying and movement underneath its paws. As a result, the dog will be very fearful and very nervous. This in turn can lead to it acting out in a way that is only natural.

There are many former purse dogs in the maltipoo rescues, and their fear and aggression is often directly related to being carried around in a purse. The constant stress and pressure of being

15

carried and thrown around can make them very skittish, and eventually, they may be inclined to bite first and to ask questions later.

On top of that, it is important to remember that small dogs tend to have very small bladders. When you are carrying your dog in a purse, it is very difficult to remember to put it down often enough to allow it to relieve itself. This can lead to unpleasant messes that you might not realize until it is too late.

In many cases, the fact that these dog purses are designed to be slung over your shoulder and across your body means that they can lead to you being fairly unaware of where you are carrying your dog and how the purse is situated. This is something that can lead to your dog getting knocked around and even injured.

When you are looking to get a maltipoo, remember that it is a real animal, not an accessory. It will always be uneasy when it is carried in such an unnatural and careless way, and even if it eventually gets used to the situation, carrying your maltipoo in a purse will never be a healthy thing to do for it.

In many cases, it is a good idea to treat your maltipoo just as you would treat a larger dog.

## 6) Veterinary Care

When it comes to veterinary care, maltipoo dogs need a bit more than medium-sized breeds.

If you are choosing a maltipoo, you are going to need to be right on top of getting it the veterinary care that it requires. This breed can be prone to injury, and there are a few health issues that are an issue for the maltipoo.

Consider whether you have the disposable income to properly care for a maltipoo.

## 7) Insurance

It is always a good idea to get pet insurance for your maltipoo. Maltipoos are delicate dogs, and you never know when disaster will strike.

When you look into pet insurance, it is usually better to put in a high monthly payment and then to pay a lower deductible. It is possible to get an excellent plan for 20 dollars or 12 pounds a month.

Start thinking about insurance as soon as you bring your dog home.

## 8) Yearly Costs

Although it is impossible to accurately estimate what the cost of owning a Maltipoo might be because unexpected medical problems might arise that would not otherwise be considered average, and you may like to buy fancy clothes for your dog every week. When thinking about sharing your life with a dog, it's important to consider more than just the daily cost of feeding your Maltipoo.

Many humans do not think about whether or not they can truly afford to care for a dog before they bring one home, and not being prepared can cause stress and problems later on.

Remember that being financially responsible for your Maltipoo is a large part of being a good guardian.

Beyond the initial investment of purchasing your Maltipoo puppy from a reputable breeder, for most guardians, owning a Maltipoo will include the costs associated with the following:

- food
- treats
- pee pads, poop bags, potty patches
- leashes and collars

- safety harnesses
- travel kennels or bags
- house training pens
- clothing
- toys
- beds
- grooming
- regular veterinary care
- obedience or dog whispering classes
- pet sitting, walking or boarding
- pet insurance
- yearly licensing
- unexpected emergencies

As you can see, depending upon where you shop, what type of food you feed your Maltipoo, what sort of veterinarian or grooming care you choose, whether or not you have pet insurance and what types of items you purchase for your Maltipoo's wellbeing, the yearly cost of owning a Maltipoo could be estimated at anywhere between $700 and $3,000 (£420 and £1,800) per year.

Other contributing factors that may have an effect on the overall yearly cost of owning a Maltipoo can include the region where you live, the accessibility of the items you need, your own lifestyle and your Maltipoo's age and individual needs.

## 9) Myths

As such a new breed, maltipoos do not have very many myths associated with them, but there are a few persistent ones.

**Myth: They will stay small if you underfeed them.**

Never underfeed an animal to keep it small. This results in malnutrition and possible death, and it is considered abuse. The size of a maltipoo is determined by its genetics.

**Myth: They do not need much exercise.**

Although they are not a working breed, maltipoos are fairly lively, and require a fair amount of exercise. Fortunately, because of their size, this exercise can often be conducted in the home.

**Myth: Maltipoos are always white.**

Many maltipoos are white. There is currently no breed standard, as such, they can also come in a range of colors, including black, brown, brindle, red, blue and apricot. You can find red maltipoo puppies for sale, apricot multipoos, and even maltipoos with various markings on them. It all depends on their ancestry and their parentage. When you are looking at a maltipoo, apricot may just be the color that wins your heart. These dogs are a soft cream color, and maltipoo apricot puppies are just endearing, even if they do not have the signature white coat. Give apricot maltipoos the same kind of love as white maltipoos get!

# 10) Trainability

Maltipoos are such a new type of dog that is difficult to give a solid answer on how trainable they are. Thanks to their poodle ancestry, which gives them impressive intelligence, they understand commands, but they can occasionally be willful.

Be willing to work with your maltipoo and to make sure that you spend a part of each day training it, socializing it and making sure that it knows how to obey.

## 11) Summing Up: Pros and Cons

Essentially, you need to find out whether this breed is the right one for you. There is no such thing as the perfect dog, but you can find a dog that is perfect for your life.

**Pro:**

Small

Low food costs

Cute

Suitable for apartment living

Active


**Con:**

Expensive unless rescued

Can bark, especially if left alone

Delicate

Prone to some genetic issues

New breed with few set standards as of yet


Think about these pros and cons and how you can integrate them into your life.

# Chapter 2) The Maltipoo as a Pet

When you are interested in getting a dog, it takes a lot of time and thought before you find the breed that is right for you. If you have no experience with maltipoos, poodles or Malteses, or you are not sure about what type of dog you want at all, it might be a good idea to figure out what the maltipoo is like as a pet.

Learn more about what your life might be like with a maltipoo, and make sure that you consider what you need to know before you bring one home. Given the fact that maltipoos live for more than ten years, purchasing a puppy is a big commitment. Make sure that you are up to the challenge.

# 1) Price

A real maltipoo is a dog that has two purebred ancestors. Given the price for high-quality dogs with known histories, this means that you will be paying a fair amount of money for your dog.

A maltipoo is a designer dog, and there is a price that comes with that. When looking over the sites of professional maltipoo breeders, you will find that it is not a shock to see asking prices between 600 and 1000 dollars, or between 360 and 600 pounds. Maltipoos with championship animals on their Maltese or their Poodle side are even more expensive.

These asking prices include things like vet support, breeding, care and health checks. Both poodles and malteses have some congenital issues that need to be weeded out, and some of the testing is designed for this very purpose.

If you cannot afford to pay the price for a maltipoo, it is far better that you avoid getting one at all. Paying a small price for a maltipoo is typically a sign that you are dealing with a backyard breeder or a breeder that is hiding something from you.

When you are looking for maltipoo puppies for sale, you need to know what you are getting. It is not the same as getting teacup Maltese puppies for sale, which have been around for a while. The teacup dog breeds have their own issues, but when you go looking for teacup dogs for sale, you know what are you getting. There are breeders out there who have crosses that may have some Maltese and some poodle ancestry in them, but you may end up paying for your cheap puppy in health issues later on down the line!

## 2) Internet Puppy Scam

Unfortunately, because the maltipoo has gained a great deal of popularity in the last few years, it has become one of the bait breeds that are often used in Internet scams.

In these scams, people set themselves up as breeders offering beautiful dogs, and once they have your money in hand, they typically disappear, leaving you with a sickly or poorly bred puppy or even no dog at all. When you are looking to buy maltipoo puppies, be very careful regarding whom you choose to give your money to.

If you are interested in getting a maltipoo puppy, the Internet will be one of the first places to take your search, but you must be wary about who you are purchasing from. Learn how you can make sure that you are buying from a real breeder.

Firstly, start by looking for a web presence. Some people believe that this is unnecessary, but a good breeder is one that treats breeding as a professional and transparent endeavor. The website is one way for you to get to know the breeder and the sires and dams that your puppy comes from, and if they are not showing their operation off, things may be looking a little suspicious.

Do not purchase maltipoos from overseas. The closer your breeder is, the better off you are going to be. The regulations that oversee the international pet trade are strict on possibly invasive exotics, but the standards get a lot looser when it comes to pets like dogs and cats. If someone is offering you an incredibly beautiful dog from overseas, skip the offer.

Find out how to get in touch with the breeder in question. Sometimes, illegitimate breeders will only give you a single email or a single method to contact them.

This means that if they are doing something illegal or unethical, they can simply ditch that mode of communication and move on when you end up unhappy with the puppy that they have sold to you.

Another thing to remember is that there are no breeders that offer quality puppies off of sites like Craigslist. If someone is offering a purebred maltipoo off of Craigslist, there are a number of things wrong.

Keep an eye on breeders who use words like mini maltipoo dogs, or teacup maltipoo for sale or toy maltipoo puppy for sale. These words don't mean much, and teacup maltipoo puppies are usually completely identical to regular maltipoo puppies. There is no size standard, even if someone is insisting on offering toy maltipoos for sale and claims to have been in business for quite some time.

Remember that a maltipoo is an expensive dog. If anyone is offering you a bargain, it isn't.

## 3) A Word About Pet Shops

When you are looking for a good place to purchase a maltipoo, the pet shop is a place that you should avoid at all costs. High quality pet shops typically do not sell anything except exotic fish and feeder animals.

The issue is that animals that make for good pets are socialized on a very regular basis. Ideally, they are handled every day and shown human affection. They get used to human voices and to touch, and they are kept in good conditions where they are allowed to exercise and play.

There are very few, if any, pet shops out there that can give a dog or puppy the amount of exercise or love that it requires. Many of the animals that come from pet shops are traumatized and have some behavioral issues to work out.

On top of that, pet shops will often refuse to tell you where they get their animals. This in itself is a problem because that usually means that they get their animals from backyard breeders or from puppy mills posing as legitimate breeders.

There are some pet shops that do not keep animals on their own, but instead will provide local rescue organizations with a place to do meet and greets with rescued animals. You may see a pen of puppies or kittens at a pet shop, but if they are associated with a rescue, there will be a very clear sign there saying so. Pet shops are ideally supply stores. They are not places where you can go to get your pet.

As you are looking for a dog that suits your needs, you'll see tempting offers in pet stores that offer you amazing prices on everything from teacup Maltese puppies to miniature Maltese litters to Maltese teacup breeds. They will offer you adorable mini Maltese dogs and plenty of toy Maltese dogs as well. However, as the reputable Maltese breeders and the veterinarians will tell you, the only place to get Maltese teacup puppies of any sort is from a breeder!

## 4) Finding a Breeder

When you are looking for a maltipoo for sale, the best place to get a maltipoo is a breeder. A good breeder is someone who offers high-quality animals for sale, and who is aware of the health issues and risks faced by breeding poorly.

When you purchase your maltipoo from a good breeder, you are getting an animal that has received good care and proper nutrition its entire life. It has been socialized to respond well to humans. You will also be able to meet the puppy's dam and perhaps the sire as well, allowing you to get an idea of what the puppy's temperament will be like when it is grown. Looking for maltipoos for sale is just like looking for Maltese teacup puppies for sale; it will help you make sure that you get a wonderful animal when it grows up.

When you are looking for maltipoos for sale, start your search online. There are a number of registries out there that provide lists of maltipoo breeders, but at this time, these lists are not screened. They can be used as a good place to start, but you will find that it is important for you to do your own research as well. When you are looking for a maltipoo breeder, remember that you should not simply look for someone with a "maltipoo puppy for sale" sign in his or her garden!

Start by looking at the list and taking note of which breeders are closest to you. Ideally, there will be a breeder in your area that you can visit. If they are local, it means that it will be much easier for you to arrange transportation, among other things.

Look at their website and get an idea of their attitudes towards breeding. How well do they understand the breed? How much experience do they have with maltipoos or with either of the parent breeds? Do they breed just maltipoos, or do they also breed other designer dogs? Your chances of a good pet typically rest with single-breed breeders.

Consider how they talk about the dogs in question. If they only talk about the fashionable quality of these dogs or if they only talk about how small they are, take a step backwards. A good breeder is someone who understands the breed and who is always looking to improve it. If they use terms like toy maltipoo or maltipoo teacup, take a step back. There is no meaning to these terms in the world of breeding maltipoos, and no standard for them.

Another thing to consider is what kind of guarantees the breeder provides. One very common thing that good breeders do is that they offer to take the animal back if you need to get rid of it.

Many breeders are very concerned about the animals that they send out into the world, and they understand that life is not always predictable. A breeder that has a guarantee about being willing to take a dog that you can no longer care for is someone who is concerned about the dogs that they produce. While it is always nice to get a very small dog, someone who is pushing the miniature maltipoo on you by saying it's the smallest around is usually an issue. Breeders who offer teacup maltipoos or who have what they call teacup maltipoos for sale often do not care about the dogs that they are producing. The same goes for people who talk about tiny toy maltipoos. Tiny toy maltipoos is a term often used to simply market these dogs.

Also be wary of any breeders who produce too many litters a year. Some small breeders only produce one or two litters a year. Other breeders, who make breeding dogs a full time job, stick with between five and six litters a year.

If your breeder boasts about handling ten or more litters a year, they might be engaging in puppy mill tactics to get the number of puppies up.

The thing to remember is that dogs are not livestock. These are companion animals that need a lot of time and a lot of devotion if they are to become sweet-natured, calm family pets. A good breeder is someone who realizes that their dogs require a lot of attention and a lot of love. Giving the dogs what they need is impossible if there are always more puppies being produced.

Once you have a short list of maltipoo puppy breeders to choose from, take a trip out to meet them. Call to talk with them about taking a quick tour and checking out how they keep their own dogs.

Depending on what breeder you end up with, you may be talking with someone who only produces a single litter a year, or you may be talking to a professional with a modern kennel set up.

In either case, you should be dealing with someone who has a lot of love for their own dogs and for the breed that they are working with.

When you go to talk to the breeder, make sure that you know how their own dogs are cared for. Ask to meet some of the dams, and see how the current litter is doing. Do not succumb to temptation and ask to take one home immediately! Just like hearing about toy maltipoo puppies and apricot teacup maltipoo puppies, be wary about a breeder who wants to put a puppy in your hands right away.

A good breeder tends to have a waiting list. A good dog is worth waiting for, and being on a waiting list means that you will be able to get to know a puppy from the time it is born. By the time you take the puppy home, you will be familiar with it and its dam.

Remember to trust your gut. If you do not get a good feeling about a breeder, that is likely a sign that something is wrong. Trust your instincts!

When you find your breeder, look for puppies that are very alert

27

and lively. They should have plenty of space to run and play, and they should be very curious about the world around them. A healthy maltipoo is a dog that feels firm in your hands, and its eyes should be bright and clear.

It should not limp at all, and its head should not wobble when it moves. A healthy maltipoo puppy has clear eyes, and there should be no discharge from its mouth, its eyes, its nose or its anus. While all dogs have an odor, your maltipoo puppy should not smell bad or unhealthy.

If you detect any signs that your maltipoo puppy is not in the peak of health, find another breeder!

## 5) Showing

Though a maltipoo might have two purebred parents, they are not purebreds themselves. The maltipoo is not recognized as a breed by neither the American Kennel Club nor the UK Kennel Club, and as a result, they are not dogs that are qualified for shows.

If you have a particularly apt and athletic maltipoo, however, you may find that you have a prime competitor for obedience trials and agility trials. These events are open to dogs of all ancestries, and due to their energy and their intelligence, maltipoos can do quite well.

## 6) The Myth of Hybrid Vigor

The theory behind hybrid vigor is that a cross between two distinct gene pools will always result in an animal that is stronger and fitter than either parent. Maltipoos are therefore often said to be genetically superior to their parents, and unfortunately, it is simply not true.

Firstly, there is no standard set for genetic superiority. This is an empty term, and more meaningful standards have never been applied.

Secondly, there is no way to know what traits you are reinforcing when you cross two purebreds. While you can end up with a dog that is stronger, healthier and more intelligent than either, you can also end up with a dog that reinforces both of the two parents' worst traits.

For example, both the Maltese and the poodle are known to be relatively intelligent breeds, with the poodle being cleverer with regards to problem solving and obedience. Theoretically, under the hybrid vigor theory, their offspring would be very intelligent.

However, there are no guarantees, and the maltipoo that you end up with could be very clever but only in certain ways. For example, it could be intelligent without being very interested in being obedient, which can be a real problem!

The truth is that while there are tests that can rule out genetic disorders, getting a crossbreed of any sort can be a bit of a gamble. You can shrink the gamble a little bit by getting to know the breeder and the parents of the dog that you are adopting. You can shrink it further by making sure that the breeder runs certain tests to rule out health problems in their puppies.

Remember that hybrid vigor is a very controversial theory, and that when you adopt a crossbreed, you never really know what you are going to be reinforcing.

## 7) Rescues

Given that maltipoos can cost from 1000 dollars or 600 pounds from a reputable breeder, you may be wondering why anyone would ever willingly give their maltipoo away!

The truth is that dogs of all types, both purebreds and mutts, are abandoned every day, and maltipoos are among that number. Maltipoos have the misfortune of being quite a popular breed right now, and there are far too many people out there who will pick one up without ever thinking of the consequences.

They may not realize how many grooming requirements a maltipoo has, or they may simply not be aware of how much care and attention a dog really requires.

With that fact in mind, it is not unusual to run into a dog at a recue shelter. There are even shelters out there that specifically deal in purebred and designer dog breeds due to the need that has been created.

While these dogs can be puppies, it is far more common for them to be half-grown dogs or adults; they are past the point of being cute, and some of that playful puppy behavior might have solidified into bad habits that were inadvertently reinforced by the owners.

It is very commendable to take on a maltipoo from a shelter, but remember to treat each animal as an individual. For example, you may be more than capable of taking on a maltipoo that is only a little past the puppy stage and simply untrained. Young dogs that are not trained can be trained with time and patience.

On the other hand, you may not be ready for an adult animal that has been abused and that has phobias and aggression or fear issues because of it.

Before you adopt any animal from a shelter, make sure that you talk to the personnel about it. Let them know what kind of time you have to devote to the animal, and tell them what your experience with animals might be. Some maltipoos emerge from troubled situations with no issues at all and can quickly become beloved family pets, while other maltipoos require some help and endless love and patience.

While it is always a good idea to get an animal from a shelter, remember that you will do more harm than good if you end up with an animal that you cannot adequately care for.

## 8) Should I Have a Maltipoo?

When you are trying to figure out if you should have a maltipoo, there are a few things that you need to keep in mind. These dogs are quite demanding of their owner's time and attention, so you must be willing to invest a lot of energy in them.

Firstly, maltipoos, like all dogs, are pack animals. They are not like cats, which can be left alone for a long workday and then are largely active at night when you are at home. Instead, Maltipoos are diurnal, meaning that they are going to be most active during normal working hours.

If you decide that you want to have a maltipoo, consider how often you are at home and for how long. If you work long hours, it might be best for you to choose another pet. Alternately, because a high-energy dog should be walked a few times a day, you may choose to hire a dog sitter or to have someone come by to keep your dog company throughout the day.

One great thing about the maltipoo is that because of its size, it makes an excellent apartment dog or housedog. However, in either case, the maltipoo still needs to be exercised, and that means that you must be willing to take the dog out on a regular basis.

Another thing to remember is that maltipoos can be barkers. This is something that can occur quite suddenly in their lives, and suddenly a relatively calm dog will turn into a ferocious barker when it is around 1 year old. This can be a serious issue even if you start trying to correct it right away, and some landlords are very strict about not having barking dogs.

Make sure that you assess your living situation before you get a maltipoo, and that you know what your options are going to be. If you live in an apartment building that is very dedicated to quiet living, a maltipoo might be a poor choice.

The maltipoo is also a dog that is lively and considered to be an extremely good family dog, but it is absolutely worth noting that because of their size, they can be quite fragile. When they are puppies, their fragility can make it dangerous for them to be around very young children. It is entirely possible for a careless, small child to injure or even kill a maltipoo puppy.

If you decide that you want a maltipoo as a family dog, wait until your children are old enough to handle small animals carefully and calmly. Most breeders recommend waiting until your children are twelve and older before getting a maltipoo.

No matter how old they are, make sure that your children know how to handle dogs, especially small dogs, before they get one. If your children are very clumsy or careless, it might be a good idea to get a dog that is simply less fragile. Maltipoos are delicate, and it does not take much rough handling to hurt them.

**Important Questions to ask**

In order to be fair to ourselves, our family and the puppy we choose to share our lives with, we humans need to take a serious look at our life both as it is today and what we envision it being in the next ten to fifteen years and then ask ourselves a few important, personal questions, and honestly answer them, before making the commitment to a puppy, including:

(1) Do I have the time and patience necessary to devote to a puppy, which will grow into a dog who needs a great deal of attention, training and endless amounts of my devotion? Keep in mind that they live, on average, for between 10 and 13 years. So you need to be able to commit to looking after your dog for that long.

(2) Do I lead a physically active, medium or low intensity life? For instance, am I out jogging the streets daily or climbing

mountains or would I rather spend my leisure time on the couch?

(3) Do I like to travel a lot? Perhaps a dog small enough to travel in the plane cabin with me is a consideration.

(4) Am I a neat freak? A non-shedding breed such as the Maltipoo would make more sense.

(5) Do I have a young, growing family that takes up all my spare time? A dog needs a lot of time and attention.

(6) Am I physically fit and healthy enough to be out there walking a dog two to three times a day, every day, rain or shine (and much more when it's just a puppy)?

(7) Can I afford the food costs and the veterinarian expenses that are part of being a conscientious dog owner?

(8) Is the decision to bring a puppy into my life a family decision, or just for the children, who will quickly lose interest?

(9) What is the number one reason why I want a dog in my life?

Once you ask yourself these important questions and honestly answer them, you will have a much better understanding of the type of puppy that would be best suited to you and your family, and whether or not it should be a Maltipoo.

If you choose the wrong dog, you will inevitably end up with an unhappy dog, which will lead to behavioral issues, which then will lead to an unhappy family. Please take the time to choose wisely.

## 9) Pet Insurance

Pet health care costs can be just as expensive as human health care costs, and one way to make some of the bills easier on you is to make sure that you have pet insurance. Pet insurance is just like insurance for people; essentially, you pay in a small amount every year or every month, and when your maltipoo has a health problem, the insurance company pays for some or all of it.

There will be a deductible that will be paid before your insurance kicks in, but then it will ideally pay for the rest. If you pay a relatively high amount on a monthly basis, you can expect your deductible to be lower.

People wonder if pet insurance is something that they should pick up for their pet, and if you have decided that you want to get a maltipoo, the answer is definitely yes.

Most people who go to breeders get a guarantee that the animal is healthy. Even a good maltipoo breeder will be the first to admit that this is a very new breed of dog, and that there are no guarantees on its health beyond what can be tested.

Make sure that your maltipoo gets the best care for its entire life. Health care for pets can be expensive, so if you have the money to set aside, make sure that you do so.

## 10) Maltipoos and Other Dogs

One of the great things about maltipoos is that they are very social animals. They are known for getting along well with humans, and that sociability usually extends to other dogs as well. While maltipoos can be introduced to other pets as adults, it is always best to socialize them when they are young.

If you are getting a maltipoo and you have another dog in the house, it is best to keep them apart at first. Keep your maltipoo puppy in an isolated room with everything it needs. This lets your maltipoo puppy get used to things slowly rather than simply plunging it into the middle of your home.

You'll likely find that your other dog or dogs will investigate the newcomer by sniffing at the door and perhaps barking. As they get more comfortable, hold your maltipoo at one end of the room while having someone else restrain the other dog at the other end of the room.

Slowly and gradually, build up their tolerance. Remember that it can take new dogs some time to get to know each other. Simply be patient.

If you have a larger dog, think seriously about whether or not you should get a maltipoo. Larger dogs with strong prey drives can hurt a maltipoo severely if they decide that the maltipoo is something to chase and pin, and even medium-sized dogs can hurt a maltipoo by playing with it too roughly.

In addition to size and prey-drive, simply think about your other dog's nature. A dog that is young and rambunctious might inadvertently hurt a maltipoo, while an older and calmer dog would be an excellent companion.

Remember that a maltipoo is not only smaller than other breeds; it is also more delicate, so introduce your maltipoo to other dogs in the household with care.

## 11) Maltipoos and Cats

Due to their small size, maltipoos are a great choice when you are looking for a dog that will not be likely to hurt your cats. A maltipoo's sociability makes them a good choice for a cat-friendly household, and when you bring home a puppy, it will be more likely to respect a cat that is bigger than it is.

Introduce your maltipoo to your cat slowly, first with a door between them and then with both animals being held at different parts of the room.

Most cats will play with maltipoos or ignore them. Remember that a rambunctious puppy can get on an older cat's nerves. To ensure that there are no scratches or fights, put up some cat shelves or some climbable furniture that will allow your cat to get away if the puppy starts to harass it.

## 12) Maltipoos as Therapy Animals and Companions

One of the most important things to remember about the maltipoo is that it is a companion animal. This is a breed that is designed to be very loving and very affectionate, and there is not much that is really independent about it.

Because of this inclination, maltipoos actually make fairly wonderful therapy animals if they are trained correctly. If you are someone that has undergone trauma of some kind or if you are someone who is feeling upset and nervous, a maltipoo might be the right answer for you.

However, it is important for you to avoid getting a maltipoo if you are worried that you cannot take care of. Some people find that the routine of caring for a dog is something that gives them purpose and an important shape to their day. Other people find the care daunting. If you are considering a therapy animal, a maltipoo may be the right choice if you remember that it is a dog, and therefore will require a certain minimum amount of care.

Take a moment to think about the fact that the maltipoo is a companion animal. It was bred to love and comfort humans, and with that in mind, remember that this is how it gets its sense of security and confidence.

A maltipoo is designed to be your best friend, so make sure that you have room for it in your life.

## 13) Licensing

You do not need a special permit or license to keep maltipoos in the US or the UK. They are not typically on the lists of restricted dogs, like the bully breeds.

However, before you purchase a puppy of any sort, always run it by your landlord first if you rent!

# 14) When to Bring Your Puppy Home

The age at which you can bring your puppy home varies from breeder to breeder. Some breeders think that 8 weeks is a fine time to bring a puppy home, while others feel that 10 weeks should be more standard.

Essentially, a maltipoo puppy that is brought home at 8 weeks will be more dependent on you and more nervous. A puppy that is brought home at 10 weeks or older will be more adventurous and confident.

Speak with your breeder about what is best for your maltipoo. They may have reasons why a puppy can be taken to your home sooner or why it should stay with its mother for a little longer.

# 15) Who Shouldn't Have a Maltipoo?

The question of who shouldn't have a maltipoo requires some thought. You should not have a maltipoo if you are going to leave it alone all the time; this is a companion animal, and although it can do well enough for short spates when you are away from home, it does need regular company.

Do not get a maltipoo if you are worried about money. This dog is quite expensive, and the veterinarian bills can pile up, especially as the dog ages.

Do not get a maltipoo if you are concerned about barking, as the breed has a bit of a reputation for baking.

Do not get a maltipoo if you want a dog with which you can wrestle. These dogs are rather delicate.

Do not get a maltipoo if you need to know exactly what your dog will look like as it grows up. Because maltipoos come from crossbreeding, this is something that is not necessarily certain. There is no set way that a maltipoo will turn out; all you can do is look at the parents and guess as best you can.

# Chapter 3) Bringing Home a Maltipoo Puppy

Getting a maltipoo puppy is very exciting, but you will discover that the process of getting ready to have one in your home is something that you should start long before the puppy comes back with you.

By being prepared for your puppy's needs, you will create a very soothing home environment that will be better for everyone. The last thing that you want is to be running around trying to find supplies late at night while you have a puppy in the car with you.

Make sure that you are prepared for your puppy's needs so that you can relax and enjoy it when you bring them home.

## 1) Puppy-Proofing the House

Young puppies are delightfully curious, but this can lead to some serious issues if you are not ready. A young puppy explores with its mouth, and you will discover that it can knock things down, chew things up and wear things out far faster than you thought possible.

Puppy-proofing your house simply means that you are going to be making your home or a section of your home safe for your puppy. For example, some people will puppy-proof a certain area, allowing the puppy out only when supervised. Other people just adjust their entire homes.

When you want to make sure that your home is puppy proof, simply start looking at things from your new puppy's point of view. If anything is within 2 feet off the ground, you can bet that your maltipoo puppy is going to be able to reach it sooner or later. This is where you have the advantage over the owners of large breeds, who need to move things even higher.

Consider the stairs when you are looking to make sure that your maltipoo puppy stays safe. A maltipoo puppy is quite small, and even if it can stretch to go up stairs, it might still take a tumble down them. Baby gates at the top and bottom of your stairs will help you keep your puppy safe, even if it is a little bit irritating to always have to open and close them when you want to use your stairs.

Be careful with electrical cords, as they are prime targets for puppyish chewing. At the very least, you will have a ruined cord, and at the very worst, your puppy might actually electrocute itself. Pull it out of the wall, move the cords from the puppy's room, or enclose the cord in chew-proof plastic tubing.

If you are keeping the puppy in the kitchen, make sure that any cabinets holding dangerous chemicals are kept latched, and that the puppy cannot pull the door open. This may seem a little extreme, but clever maltipoo puppies can crawl into the oddest places, and they can knock over plenty of dangerous chemicals.

Pick up small items, and be very diligent about keeping the floors clean. Your puppy can eat a wide variety of things that it shouldn't, and even innocuous items can harm it. Things like string, rubber bands, thumbtacks and paperclips can really hurt your puppy so be very, very careful.

One place that often gets neglected in terms of puppy safety is the garage and the yard. If your dog is going to have any access to these spots, think about some of the dangers. The garage is full of dangerous chemicals, antifreeze being among the worst offenders. The sweet taste of antifreeze draws maltipoos to it, and this can lead to poisoning. Be sure that you keep all of these dangerous chemicals away from your puppy and on a shelf or in a cabinet.

Another thing to remember is that there are plenty of plants in a normal garden that are dangerous to your maltipoo puppy. There will be more about that later on in the book. Remember that most houseplants are poisonous to dogs, though whether they will actually kill your puppy or just make it sick is a toss-up.

Most puppies will be a curious bundle of energy, which means that they will get to everything within their reach.

As a responsible puppy guardian, you will want to provide a safe environment for them, which means eliminating all sources of danger, similar to what you would do for a curious toddler.

Be aware that your Maltipoo puppy will want to touch, sniff, taste, investigate and closely inspect every electrical cord, every closet, every nook and cranny of your home and everything you may have left lying about on the floor.

Power cords can be found in just about every room in the home and to a teething puppy, these may look like irresistible and fun chew toys. Make sure that you tuck all power cords securely out of your puppy's reach or enclose them inside a chew-proof PVC tube.

**Kitchen**: first of all, there are many human foods that can be harmful to dogs, therefore, your kitchen should always be strictly off limits to your puppy any time you are preparing food. Calmly send them out of the kitchen any time you are in the kitchen, and they will quickly get the idea that this area is off limits to them.

**Bathroom**: bathroom cupboards and drawers or the side of a bathtub where you may leave your shaving supplies can hold many dangers for a young and curious Maltipoo puppy.

Kleenex, cotton swabs, Q-tips, toilet paper, razors, pills and soap left within your puppy's reach are an easy target that could result in an emergency visit to your veterinarian's office.

Family members need to put shampoos, soap, facial products, makeup and accessories out of reach or safely inside a cabinet or drawer.

**Bedroom**: if you don't keep your shoes, slippers and clothing safely behind doors, you may find that your puppy has claimed them for their new chew toys. Be vigilant about keeping everything in its safe place, including jewelry, hair ties, bills, coins, and other items small enough for them to swallow in containers or drawers, and secure any exposed cords or wires.

If you have children, make sure that they understand that, especially while your puppy is going through their teething stage, they must keep their rooms tidy and leave nothing that could cause a choking problem to the puppy on the floor or within their reach.

**Living Room**: we humans often spend many hours in our cozy gathering places to watch movies or play games, and often the living areas of our homes will have many items that are very enticing for a curious and teething puppy, such as books, magazines, pillows, iPods, TV remotes and more.

You will want to keep your home free of excess clutter and remain vigilant about straightening up and putting things out of sight that could be tempting to your puppy.

**Office**: we humans often spend a great deal of time in our home offices, which means that our puppy will want to be there, too, and they will be curious about all the items an office has to offer, including papers, books, magazines, and electrical cords.

Although your puppy might think that rubber bands or paper clips are fun to play with, allowing these items to be within your puppy's reach could end up being a fatal mistake if your puppy swallows them.

**Plants**: these are also a very tempting target for your puppy's teeth, so you will want to keep them well out of their reach. If you have floor plants, they will need to be moved to a shelf or counter or placed behind a closed door until your curious fur friend grows out of the habit of putting everything in its mouth. Also keep in mind that many common houseplants are poisonous to dogs.

**Garage and Yard**: there are obvious as well as subtle dangers that could seriously harm or even kill a Maltipoo puppy that are often found in the garage or yard. Some of these might include antifreeze, gasoline, fertilizers, rat and mice poison, snail and slug poison, weed killer, paint, cleaners and solvents, grass seed, bark mulch and various insecticides.

If you are storing any of these toxic substances in your garage or garden shed, make sure that you keep all such bottles, boxes, or containers inside a locked cabinet, or stored on high shelves that your puppy will not be able to reach. Even better, choose not to use toxic chemicals anywhere in your home or yard.

**Puppy Hazard Home Inspection**

Every conscientious puppy guardian needs to take a serious look around the home not just from the human eye level, but also from the eye level of a Maltipoo puppy. This means literally crawling around your floors.

Your puppy has a much lower vantage point than you do when standing, therefore, there may be items in your environment that could potentially be harmful to a Maltipoo puppy that a human might not notice unless you get down on the floor and take a really good look.

# 2) Finding Pet Services

Once you know that you are getting a maltipoo, before you bring it home, it is important to look around for the people who will help you give your dog great care.

Firstly, make sure that you know a good veterinarian. There are usually quite a few veterinarians in the area, but there will always be a few that stand out. Call around and find out who has experience with small dogs. It would be great if they have experience with maltipoos, but in general, remember that this is still a fairly new breed. It is helpful if they have worked with Malteses and poodles; the maltipoo's parent breeds.

## 3) Talking to Your Children

If you are bringing your maltipoo into a house with children, it is very important that you spend some time getting your children used to the idea of having a dog as small and as fragile as a maltipoo.

A maltipoo is not the best dog in the world to purchase for your children, especially if they are young or clumsy. When you want a dog that will be more of a companion for active children, you might want to look into getting a larger, sturdier animal.

When you are bringing a maltipoo to a home with children, speak seriously with your children about the idea that the maltipoo is very fragile. Even a small amount of careless handling can lead to some serious injuries, and when you have a dog this small in the house, it is important to do things like watch when you close the door or where the runners on a rocking chair are going.

Make sure that your children know that a maltipoo is not a toy. When they want to play with the maltipoo, they must handle it very gently, and they must support the dog's entire body.

Show your children how to pick up a small dog. Essentially, one hand goes around the dog's chest to prevent it from jumping, and another hand goes underneath the dog's hindquarters to keep it from slipping away. The more solid a hold you have on the dog, the happier it will be in general. Remind your children that the maltipoo will be very nervous and scared when it first comes into the house, and that they need to remain calm.

## 4) Preparing Other Pets

If you have other pets in the house, it is often a good idea to get them used to the idea of the maltipoo pup before you bring it home. If at all possible, ask the breeder for a towel or a blanket that the maltipoo has slept on or otherwise used. This allows you to bring the item home and to make sure that your other animals are getting used to the new puppy's scent.

In some cases, especially when you are dealing with a rescue maltipoo, you can bring your own dogs out to meet the new puppy. This is something that can make a huge difference to their eventual interaction. This can tell you if your older dog will tolerate a newcomer and it can help you figure out how easy the transition may be.

## 5) Getting a Puppy Room

Many people decide that a maltipoo puppy is simply too small to be allowed full run of the house at first, and they choose to create a puppy room that is ideal for the puppy. This is something that can help your puppy get used to the house, and it only takes a little bit of setting up.

In the first place, decide where the puppy room is going to be. Remember that your puppy is very young and small, and so you should not choose a room that is out of the way or where people will not be able to see it on a very regular basis.

One great option is to simply use baby gates and other fencing to create a small puppy area in a room that gets a moderate amount of traffic, whether that is the living room or the kitchen. Fence out a certain area for the puppy, and make sure that it is large enough for a bed, the food dishes and some toys.

You can remove the puppy from the play area for some interaction if you wish, and then the puppy can be put in its area when it is tired out or when you need to do something else.

Remember that maltipoos are a bit sensitive to temperature, and because of that, you are going to need to think about how you can make sure that the area in question is draft free. Make sure that you figure out if there are any drafts in the area, and if there are, find a way to block them.

Check the puppy room and make sure that there is nothing that the puppy can grab or break at all. This is why having a dedicated area for your puppy works so well.

## 6) Should I Get More Than One?

Maltipoos are dogs, and as such, they will always love having a friend. If you are going to be busy on a regular basis, getting two is a good choice, but remember that two maltipoo puppies are essentially double the trouble!

If you are worried about your maltipoo being lonely, it might be better for you to choose another pet rather than to add another maltipoo to the mix!

## 7) Boy or Girl?

At this point, there does not seem to be a difference between male and female maltipoos aside from the standard differences between male and female dogs. For the most part, female maltipoos tend to be more independent though slightly more trainable than their male counterparts, Males are more outgoing, but a little more distractible.

It is thought in some places that females make better companions for children, but there is nothing to say that you won't pick a male puppy that is incredibly sweet and loving as well.

At the end of the day, training and socialization has far more to do with whether this dog is a good choice for you than sex does.

## 8) Common Mistakes to Avoid

### a) Sleeping in Your Bed

Many people make the mistake of allowing a crying puppy to sleep with them in their bed, and while this may help to calm and comfort a new puppy, it will set a dangerous precedent that can result in behavioral problems later on in their life.

In addition, a tiny Maltipoo puppy can easily be crushed by a sleeping human body.

As much as it may pull on your heart strings to hear your new Maltipoo puppy crying the first couple of nights on their own, a little tough love at the beginning will help them to learn to both love and respect you as their leader.

### b) Picking Them Up at the Wrong Time

Never pick your puppy up if they display fear or growl at an object or person, because this will be rewarding them for unbalanced behavior.

Instead, your puppy needs to be gently corrected by you, with firm and calm energy so that they learn not to react with fear or aggression.

### c) Playing Too Hard or Too Long

Many humans play too hard or allow their children to play too long with a young puppy. You need to remember that a young puppy tires very easily and, especially during the critical growing phases of their young life, they need their rest.

## d) Hand Play

Always discourage your Maltipoo puppy from chewing or biting your hands, or any part of your body for that matter. If you allow them to do this when they are puppies, they will want to continue to do so when they have strong jaws and adult teeth and this is not acceptable behavior for any breed of dog.

Do not get into the habit of playing the *"hand"* game, where you rough up the puppy and slide them across the floor with your hands, because this will teach your puppy that your hands are play things.

When your puppy is teething, they will naturally want to chew on everything within reach, and this will include you. As cute as you might think it is, this is not an acceptable behavior and you need to gently, but firmly, discourage the habit.

A light flick with a finger on the end of a puppy nose, combined with a firm "NO" when they are trying to bite human fingers will discourage them from this activity.

## e) Distraction and Replacement

When your puppy tries to chew on your hand, foot, or your clothing, or anything else that is not fair game, you need to firmly and calmly tell them "no", and then distract them by replacing what they are not supposed to be chewing with their chew toy.

Make sure that you happily praise them every time they choose the toy to chew on.

If the puppy continues chewing on you, remove yourself from the equation by getting up and walking away. If they are really persistent, put them inside their kennel with a favorite chew toy until they calm down.

Always praise your puppy when they stop inappropriate behavior so that they begin to understand what they can and cannot do.

## 9) The First Weeks With Your Puppy

You will begin bonding with your Maltipoo puppy from the very first moment you bring them home from the breeders.

This is the time when your puppy will be the most distraught as they will no longer have the guidance, warmth and comfort of their mother or their other litter mates, and you will need to take on the role of being your new puppy's center of attention.

Be patient and kind with them as they are learning you are now their new center of the universe.

Your daily interaction with your puppy during play sessions and especially your disciplined exercises, including going for walks on a leash, and teaching commands and tricks, will be the best bonding opportunities.

Do not make the mistake of thinking that *"bonding"* with your new puppy can only happen if you are playing or cuddling together, because the very best bonding happens when you are kindly teaching rules and boundaries.

### a) The First Night

Before you go to the breeder's to pick up your new Maltipoo puppy, vacuum your floors and do a last minute check of every room to make sure that everything that could be a puppy hazard is carefully tucked away out of sight and that nothing is left on the floor or low down on shelves where a curious puppy might get into trouble.

Close most of the doors inside your home, so that there are just one or two rooms that the puppy will have access to.

You have already been shopping and have everything you need, so get out a puppy pee pad and have it at the ready when you bring your new furry friend home.

Also have your soft bed(s) in an area where you will be spending most of your time and where they will be easily found by your puppy. If you have already purchased a soft toy, leave it in your puppy's soft bed, or take the toy with you when you go to pick up your puppy.

NOTE: take either your hard-sided kennel or your soft-sided "Sherpa" travel bag with you when going to bring your new Maltipoo puppy home, and make sure that it is securely fastened to the seat of your vehicle with the seatbelt system and lined with a puppy pee pad.

Even though you will be tempted to hold your new Maltipoo puppy in your lap on the drive home, this is a very dangerous place for them to be, in case of an accident.

Place them inside their kennel or bag, which will be lined with soft towels and perhaps even a warm, towel wrapped hot water bottle, and close the door. If you have a friend who can drive for you, sit beside them in the back seat, and if they cry on the way home, remind them that they are not alone with your soft, soothing voice.

Before bringing your new Maltipoo puppy inside your home, take them to the place where you want them to relieve themselves and try to wait it out long enough for them to at least go pee.

Then bring them inside your home and introduce them to the area where their food and water bowls will be kept, in case they are hungry or thirsty.

Let them wander around, sniffing and checking out their new surroundings and gently encourage them to follow you wherever you go.

Show them where the puppy pee pad is located and place it near the door where you will exit to take them outside to relieve themselves. Many pee pads are scented to encourage a puppy to pee, and if they do, happily praise them.

Show them where their hard-sided kennel is (in your bedroom) and put them inside with the door open while you sit on the floor in front and quietly encourage them to relax inside their kennel.

Depending on the time of day when you bring your new Maltipoo puppy home for the first time, practice this kennel exercise several times throughout the day, and if they will take a little treat each time you encourage them to go inside their kennel, this will help to further encourage the behavior of wanting to go inside.

After they have had their evening meal, take them outside approximately 20 minutes later to relieve themselves, and when they do, make sure you are very enthusiastic with your praise and perhaps even give a little treat.

So far your Maltipoo puppy has only been allowed in several rooms of your home, as you have kept the other doors closed, so keep it this way for the first few days.

Before it is time for bed, again take your puppy outside for a very short walk to the same place where they last relieved themselves and make sure that they go pee before bringing them back inside.

Before bed, prepare your Maltipoo puppy's hot water bottle and wrap it in a towel so that it will not be too hot for them, and place it inside their hard-sided kennel (in your bedroom).

Turn the lights down low and invite your puppy to go inside their kennel and if they seem interested, perhaps give them a soft toy to have inside with them. Let them walk into the kennel at their own pace and when they do, give them a little treat (if they are interested) and encourage them to snuggle down to sleep while you are sitting on the floor in front of the kennel.

Once they have settled down inside their kennel, close the door, go to your bed and turn all the lights off. It may help your puppy to sleep during their first night home if you can play quiet, soothing music in the background.

If they start to cry or whine, stay calm and have compassion because this is the first time in their young life when they do not have the comfort of their mother or their litter mates. Do not let them out of their kennel, simply reassure them with your calm voice that they are not alone until they fall asleep.

## b) The First Week

During the first week, you and your new Maltipoo puppy will be getting settled into the new routine, which will involve you getting used to your puppy's needs as they also get used to your usual schedule.

Be as consistent as possible with your waking and sleeping routine, getting up and going to bed at the same time each day, so that it will be easier for your puppy to get into the flow of their new life.

First thing in the morning, remove your puppy from their kennel and take them immediately outside to relieve themselves at the place where they last went to pee.

At this time, if you are teaching them to ring a doorbell to go outside, let them ring the bell before you go out the door with them, whether you are carrying them, or whether they are walking out the door on their own.

**NOTE**: during the first week, you may want to carry your puppy outside first thing in the morning as they may not be able to hold it for very long once waking up.

When you bring them back inside, you can let them follow you so they get used to their new leash and/or harness arrangement.

Be very careful not to drag your puppy if they stop or pull back on the leash. If they refuse to walk on the leash, just hold the tension toward you (without pulling) while encouraging them to walk toward you, until they start to move forward again.

Now it will be time for their first feed of the day, and after they have finished eating, keep an eye on the clock, because you will want to take them outside to relieve themselves in about 20 minutes.

When your puppy is not eating or napping, they will be wanting to explore and have little play sessions with you and these times will help you bond with your puppy more and more each day.

As their new guardian, it will be your responsibility to keep a close eye on them throughout the day, so that you can notice when they need to relieve themselves and either take them to their pee pad or take them outside.

You will also need to make sure that they are eating and drinking enough throughout the day, so set regular feeding times at least three times a day.

Also set specific times in the day when you will take your puppy out for a little walk on a leash and harness, so that they are not only going outside when they need to relieve themselves, but they are also learning to explore their new neighborhood with you beside them.

When your Maltipoo puppy is still very young, you will not want to walk for a long time as they will get tired easily, so keep your walks to no more than 15 or 20 minutes during your first week and if they seem tired or cold, pick them up and carry them home.

# Chapter 4) Supply Basics

One of the important things to remember about puppies of all kinds is that they have a lot of needs that you will need to provide for. There is a great deal of shopping to be done before your puppy comes home, and the more shopping you do early on, the more relaxed your puppy's integration into your home is going to be. Check out this shopping list and make sure that you have every single need accounted for.

## 1) Bed

Your puppy's bed is going to be the place where it sleeps. No matter how much your puppy whimpers, do not let it sleep with you. Having a bed will give your puppy a place to claim as its own. Remember that pet beds come in all sizes, and that for a maltipoo, you are likely going to want the smallest bed that you can find. Even then, it might be rather large for your maltipoo pup, so consider lining it with a few towels to make it cozier.

US Price: 20 dollars / UK Price 12 pounds

## 2) Bowls

Maltpoo puppies need both food and water bowls, and you will find that the best option is going to be bowls that are made out of stainless steel. This is a good way to cut down on potential tear staining and to ensure the absolute minimum amount of bacteria buildup. Stainless steel bowls are easily sanitized with soap and hot water.

US Price: 10 dollars / UK Price 6 pounds

## 3) Collar/Harness

When you bring your puppy home, it will likely be too small to need a collar with ID. A collar with ID essentially ensures that your dog will be returned to you if it goes roaming, and puppies that young in general will be mostly housebound or restricted to the yard for the most part.

However, whenever your puppy does leave the home, be sure to put on a collar with the right ID information on the tag. Remember that the collar should be fit so that you can ease two fingers between your dog's neck and the collar for the best results.

For maltipoos, make sure that you stick with a harness first. Harness do not put pressure on these puppy's delicate throats, so when you go for a walk, keep the collar on, but add a harness so that you can attach the leash.

US Price Collar: 8 dollars

UK Price Collar: 2 pounds

US Price Harness: 15 dollars

UK Price Harness: 10 pounds

## 4) Leash

Leashes allow you to keep your maltipoo puppy near you when you are out and about. Even if you mostly intend to carry your puppy, a leash is an important safety mechanism. Consider a retractable leash so that neither you nor your puppy trip over the excess.

US Price: 12 dollars

UK Price: 4 pounds

## 5) Puppy Food

Just like human infants need baby food, puppies need puppy food. This food is designed to be full of nutrients and proteins; things that help your maltipoo grow. There are several great brands to choose from, but you should always ask your veterinarian what they recommend. Good nutrition at this early age is something that can preclude difficult issues later on, so take a keen interest in what your puppy eats.

US Price: 50 dollars/30 pounds

UK Price: 33 pounds for 15 kg

## 6) Toys

Your puppy is just like a little kid, and like a little kid, your maltipoo pup will want to play! When you want to keep your puppy's play interesting and exciting, consider the toys that you want to bring home. To prevent the possibility of choking, remember that your dog's toys should be hard and fairly indestructible. Do not give your maltipoo puppy anything that is small enough to swallow or anything that will shatter under your puppy's jaws.

Puppies tend to love toys that make sounds, but always remember that if you purchase your puppy a toy with a noisemaker in it, you will be hearing it all day, every day.

US Price: 20 dollars

UK Price: 12 pounds

## 7) Puppy Pads

When you first bring your puppy home, puppy pads are a great way to make sure that any accidents that occur during housebreaking are easily cleaned up.

US Price: 50 dollars

UK Price: 25 pounds

## 8) Baggies/Baggie Dispensers

When you go walking with your puppy, it is a good idea to have baggies on hand to pick up the feces. Simply keeping a baggie dispenser by your door that is always full of baggies can make a huge difference to your convenience.

US Price: 10 dollars

UK Price: 6 pounds

## 9) Grooming Supplies

When you are invested in your dog's health, you need to make sure that you have the supplies to keep it well groomed. While professional grooming is an essential part of maltipoo care, you will discover that you can handle many day-to-day items on your own.

When it comes to taking care of your maltipoo's coat, make sure that you consider getting a brush and a comb at the very least. Talk with your breeder about what kind of coat your maltipoo has and what the best brushes are going to be. The mix of poodle and Maltese can create a few different fur types, and they have different needs.

Also make sure that you have scissors with blunted tips that you can use to cut out mats or to remove knots, and that you also have nail clippers designed for dogs in your grooming kit.

Finally, make sure that you have cornstarch, which you can use to staunch bleeding from a toenail that has been trimmed too short.

US Price: 30 dollars

UK Price: 15 pounds

## 10) Toothbrush/Toothpaste

Brushing your maltipoo puppy's teeth is a good way to keep it healthy and to prevent dental issues, and getting started with this good habit as soon as your puppy comes home is essential.

Buy a toothbrush and toothpaste that is right for a dog at your local pet store and check out the different flavors of toothpaste that might be available. It is often a good idea to buy a selection to see what your dog might like.

US Price: 5 dollars

UK Price: 5 pounds

## 11) Dog Carrier

Your maltipoo puppy will need to be making trips to the veterinarian, and if you travel yourself, you will discover that it is far better to have your puppy in a carrier rather than bouncing around loose in the car.

When you are choosing a dog carrier, you will find that it is essential to ensure that the carrier is sized to your dog. Choose a small carrier for your maltipoo puppy, which after all will never grow to be very large.

US Price: 30 dollars

UK Price: 15 pounds

## 12) Towels

Maltipoo puppies make messes, and maltipoo puppies need to stay warm. These two things together mean that having a lot of old towels around is a great idea when it comes to keeping your maltipoo puppy in good health.

Go to a thrift store or a secondhand store and simply purchase a lot of old ragged towels. They are going to be great for cleaning your puppy, for keeping it warm and a number of other tasks. Remember that they don't have to look pretty; they just have to ensure that your puppy stays comfortable.

If you intend to crate your maltipoo puppy, make sure that you purchase a crate that is suitable for the size of your puppy. Do not purchase a larger cage because it is on sale or because you think that your puppy needs the room.

The right crate will allow your puppy to turn around comfortably in it while also having enough room for the food bowl, the water bowl and a few toys.

The crate should ideally be made of stainless steel, and you should line the bottom of the cage with towels and other padding so that the dog will be less inclined to develop foot issues.

Remember that the crate is going to be your puppy's home in many ways, so choose wisely and make sure that you look into choosing a cage that will last.

# Chapter 5) Maltipoo Care

When you are interested in picking up a maltipoo as a pet, you will discover that you are looking at a dog that requires a fair amount of care. The breed is still new enough that we are learning about the best ways to care for these lovable dogs, but at this point, there are a few sure things that you need to count on. Consider what it takes to care for a maltipoo before you choose to bring one home.

## 1) Feeding

When you want to make sure that your maltipoo is healthy, one of the first things that you need to think about is what you are feeding it. It is remarkably easy to overfeed small dogs, and it is important for you to consider what your dog needs, and not simply what the label on the bag says.

It is worth speaking with your veterinarian when you go in to get your puppy its shots. Maltipoos can take after their poodle ancestry or their Maltese ancestry, and as a result, you will find that there may be some particularities your veterinarian wants you to look out for.

In general, when your dog is a year old or younger, you will be feeding it about an ounce of food for every pound the dog weighs every day. If a young Maltese weighs 5 pounds or 2.2 kilograms, you would feed it five ounces or about 150 grams of food every day. This amount of food might seem like a lot, but remember that you are feeding a growing animal.

After your maltipoo is a year old, it can graduate to eating about ½ ounce of food per pound per day. This may seem like a drastic reduction, but the truth is that this is the difference between a young animal and an adult. Depending on how well the dog is thriving and growing, you may be able to reduce its food sooner or you might want to keep it on a heavier diet for another few months.

Essentially, this rule of thumb requires that you cut down the dog's feed when it starts to grow.

When you are thinking about feeding your maltipoo, speak to your veterinarian about what food they recommend. While maltipoos are not prone to issues that require a special diet, you never know when yours might be a special case.

When you go looking for dog food yourself, look for a food that will tell you what is in it, and what the percentage of items might be. Dogs are omnivorous, but eating a diet that is too high in grains like wheat and corn can result in allergies later on down the line.

Make sure that meat is the first ingredient on your dog food's list, but remember that it is not always enough. If the list of ingredients reads something like "chicken, corn, soy and wheat," there is a chance that the chicken may make up the largest single percentage of the food, but it is quickly overwhelmed by corn, soy and wheat.

Some people also find that maltipoos do very well on a diet of homemade dog food. While this is likely the very best option for maltipoos, it can be time consuming and expensive for the owner. However, you will also realize that this might be less expensive than you think since your maltipoo is smaller than other dogs!

While there are definitely dog food recipes online, it is in your best interests to work with your veterinarian on developing the right dog food for your particular dog or puppy.

## 2) Exercise

Maltipoos are little bundles of energy, and though this is most obvious when they are puppies, they remain energetic all their lives. Unlike larger breeds that become couch potatoes as they age, maltipoos have an eternal puppy nature, and they will always want to play!

Most maltipoos need about 30 minutes of exercise per day. This does not mean that you have to walk them 30 minutes a day. As a matter of fact, this can even be a little tough on their joints.

Instead of extended activity, give them little ten-minute sessions of play. Throw them a ball, teach them to try to find something that you have hidden or spend some time training them.

A maltipoo is very energetic, but also remember that it is a very small dog. You cannot take it running and expect it to keep up, and you will find that if you try, you have to carry it back!

Find games that you can play with your maltipoo and make sure that you play them regularly. Some maltipoos love to play tug-of-war, but if you decide to play this game, always play it with the same toy. The last thing that you want is a dog that thinks it's a good idea to play it with your socks or your shoes when you are in a hurry!

## 3) Weather

Maltipoos are fairly delicate dogs, and they are not adjusted to neither the cold nor the heat. When you start to feel chilled, dress your maltipoo in a sweater or a dog coat to keep him warm. When the temperature dips below freezing, it is time to keep your beloved pet indoors!

Maltipoos can also get overheated fairly quickly. When the temperature goes above 85 degrees Fahrenheit or 30 degrees Celsius, skip the cardio activity and simply bring your dog outside for bathroom breaks.

The nice thing about maltipoos is that they can get a lot of exercise while they are indoors. Some of them will chase streamers on wands like cats, while others delight in playing fetch in a long hallway.

Remember that a maltipoo does not have any more defenses against the cold than you do. They are not like huskies or malamutes, which were bred for northern climes. If you need a coat outside, so does your dog, and when the temperatures drop, you should also consider booties for the dog's feet as well.

Use common sense when you are bundling up your dog for the chilly morning or the humid afternoons.

## 4) Teething

Maltipoo puppies are born without teeth, but very quickly thereafter, they will start to grow small teeth that are typically milk teeth. By the time you bring your maltipoo puppy home, it will have a complete set of 28 milk teeth. Much like humans, however, maltipoo puppies will lose their milk teeth, and get adult teeth as they grow up.

For most maltipoos, the first signs of their adult teeth start to appear around the age of 4 months or so. The incisors are the first teeth to grow in, and this process can range from being mildly irritating to painful.

When your puppy starts teething, there are many things that you can do to help it. Start by offering your puppy plenty of chew toys. Chewing at this stage is very natural because it allows the puppy to relieve some of the pain with the pressure from chewing. However, this means that your puppy might be a little indifferent to what it is chewing on, and you can lose some shoes, purses or furniture this way!

Another thing to remember is that you can often give puppies hard rubber toys that can be chilled in your refrigerator. Cold will numb the pain as your puppy chews away, and this can make sure that your puppy stays calm.

Make sure that you are keeping up any tooth brushing that you have managed to establish at this point. Chewing and teething should be a time when you are taking better care of your puppy's teeth. Teething lasts about two months, until the puppy is between six and seven months old. This can feel like quite a trying period, but it will be over before you know it.

# 5) Neutering and Spaying

When you are choosing a maltipoo, remember that you are choosing a dog that is not registered with any standard breed registry or kennel club. Because of that, you will find that your dog has very few opportunities to be bred for anything near a profit. This means that unless your circumstances are exceptional, you should likely neuter or spay your maltipoo puppy rather than leaving it unaltered and hoping for successful breeding.

Remember that breeding is an endeavor that requires time and a great deal of effort. The only people who make money off of breeding are legitimate breeders who spend years looking into how to improve the breed and puppy mills, which turn out hundreds of poorly bred dogs to supply the demands at pet stores.

If you are simply purchasing a companion animal, there are many reasons to have your maltipoo spayed or neutered.

Both spaying and neutering are very simple operations that remove your maltipoo's drive and ability to reproduce. They are standard operations, and they are very safe.

Male maltipoos that have been neutered are markedly less aggressive and less inclined to mark their territory. They become less competitive with other dogs, and they are more likely to bond closely with their human owners.

Female maltipoos that have been spayed do not go into heat the way that unaltered females do. They are significantly less nervous, and they do not cry and bark the way that females in heat do.

Both male and female dogs are less inclined to roam when they have been altered, and they are significantly more calm and sedentary. They are less likely to want to slip the leash when they smell a possible mate nearby, and they will not try like crazy to get out of the house to go wandering.

Most breeders will ask for a signed statement from you stating that you will get the puppy spayed or neutered when your veterinarian deems it appropriate, and you should keep this in mind. Spaying or neutering your pet is a good way to keep it safe or healthy. These procedures cut down or eliminate certain types of cancer in your dog, and they only need to happen once. Take responsibility and make sure

## a) What is Neutering?

Neutering is a surgical procedure, carried out by a licensed veterinarian surgeon, which renders a male dog unable to reproduce.

In males, the surgery is also referred to as *"castration"* because the procedure entails the removal of the young dog's testicles. When the testicles are removed, what is left behind is an empty scrotal sac (which used to contain the puppy's testicles) and this empty sac will soon shrink in size until it is no longer noticeable.

## b) Neutering Males

Neutering male Maltipoo puppies before they are six months of age can help to ensure that they will be less likely to suffer from obesity as they grow older.

Neutering can also mean that a male Maltipoo will be less likely to have the urge to wander.

Furthermore, waiting until a male Maltipoo is older than six months before having them neutered could mean that they will experience the effects of raging testosterone that will drive them to escape their yards by any means necessary to search out females to mate with.

Non-neutered males also tend to spray or mark territory far more; both inside and outside the home, and during this time can start to display aggressive tendencies toward other dogs as well as people.

## c) What is Spaying?

In female puppies, sterilization, referred to as *"spaying"* is a surgical procedure carried out by a licensed veterinarian to prevent the female dog from becoming pregnant and to stop regular heat cycles.

The sterilization procedure is much more involved for a female puppy (than for a male), as it requires the removal of both ovaries and the uterus by incision into the puppy's abdominal cavity. The uterus is also removed during this surgery to prevent the possibility of it becoming infected later on in life.

While it can sometimes be difficult to find the definitive answer about when is the best time to neuter or spay your young Maltipoo, as there are varying opinions on this topic, one thing that most veterinarians do agree on is that earlier spaying or neutering, between 4 and 6 months of age, is a better choice than waiting.

Spaying or neutering surgeries are carried out under general anesthesia.

More dogs are being neutered at younger ages, so speak with your veterinarian and ask for their recommendations regarding the right age to spay or neuter your Maltipoo.

## d) Effects on Aggression

Intact (non-neutered) males and females are more likely to display aggression related to sexual behavior than neutered animals. Fighting, particularly in males, is less common after neutering.

The intensity of other types of aggression, such as irritable aggression in females, will be totally eliminated by spaying.

While neutering or spaying is not a treatment for aggression, it can certainly help to minimize the severity and escalation of aggressiveness and is often the first step towards resolving an aggressive behavior problem.

## e) Spaying Females

Preferably, female Maltipoo puppies should be spayed before their very first estrus or heat cycle. Females in heat often appear more agitated and irritable, sleep and eat less and some may become extremely aggressive towards other dogs.

Spaying female puppies before their first heat pattern can eliminate these hormonal stressors and reduce the likelihood of mammary glandular tumors. Early spaying also protects against various other potential concerns, such as uterine infections.

## f) Effects on General Temperament

Many dog owners often become needlessly worried that a neutered or spayed dog will lose their vigor. Rest assured that a dog's personality or energy level will not be modified by neutering, and in fact, many unfavorable qualities resulting from hormonal impact may resolve after surgery.

Your Maltipoo will certainly not come to be less caring or cheerful, and neither will it resent you because you are not denying your dog any essential encounters. You will, however, be acting as an accountable, informed, and caring Maltipoo owner.

Further, there is little evidence to suggest that the nature of a female Maltipoo will improve after having a litter of puppies.

It is important that you do not place your own psychological needs or concerns onto your Maltipoo puppy, because there is no gain to be had from permitting sexual activity in either male or female canines.

It is not *"abnormal"* or *"mean"* to manage a puppy's reproductive activity by having them sterilized. Rather, it is unkind not to neuter or spay a dog and there are many benefits of having this procedure carried out.

### g) Effects on Escape and Roaming

A neutered or spayed Maltipoo is less likely to wander. Castrated male dogs have the tendency to patrol smaller sized, outdoor areas and are less likely to participate in territorial conflicts with perceived opponents.

NOTE: a Maltipoo that has actually already had successful escapes from the yard may continue to wander after they are spayed or neutered.

### h) Effects on Problem Elimination

An unsterilized dog may urinate or defecate inside the home or in other undesirable areas in an attempt to make territorial claims, relieve anxiety, or advertise their available reproductive status.

While neutering or spaying a Maltipoo puppy after they have already begun to inappropriately eliminate or mark territory to announce their sexual availability to other dogs will reduce the more powerful urine odor as well as eliminate the hormonal factors, once this habit has begun, the undesirable behavior may continue to persist after neutering or spaying.

## i) Possible Weight Gain

While metabolic changes that occur after spaying or neutering can cause some Maltipoo puppies to gain weight, often the real culprit for any weight gain is the human who feels guilty for subjecting their puppy to any kind of pain and therefore attempt to make themselves feel better by feeding more treats or meals to their Maltipoo companion.

If you are concerned about weight gain after neutering or spaying a Maltipoo puppy, simply adjust their food and treat consumption as needed.

It is a very simple process to change your Maltipoo's food intake according to their physical demands and how they look, and if your Maltipoo puppy's daily exercise and level of activity has not changed after they have been spayed or neutered, there will likely be no change in food management necessary.

# 6) Caring for a Rescue Maltipoo

It is a sad fact, but there are many people who take on beautiful maltipoos and then find out that they cannot care for them. Rescue maltipoos are often older puppies or adult dogs, and they have come from a variety of home situations. Some are poorly trained or not trained at all, others have been abused and have undergone a great deal of stress in their lives. Others are well behaved and sweet-tempered. It is difficult to know what you are getting with a rescue.

When you are looking to adopt a rescue maltipoo, the best way for you to get started is to spend some time with the rescue organization. They will likely have a full write-up of the maltipoo's history and any known issues. When they tell you that a maltipoo is challenging or needs a lot of love and care, believe them.

Make sure that you get a good idea of what the maltipoo's health needs are. Some maltipoos from abusive situations are frailer than their luckier cousins and they may require lifetime medical care even when they are very young.

If you can, spend some time with the maltipoo at the rescue where it is staying. Get to know the dog over the course of a few days so that when you go to take it home, you are not doing so as a complete stranger.

Do not be offended if your maltipoo rescue is very skittish. Dogs are socialized to want and need our love and approval, but bad experiences can render it unable to act on that need. Do not grab your rescue maltipoo and pull it towards you.

When you bring your maltipoo home, it is a good idea to set it up in its own room. You might want to introduce your rescue to the entire house, but it will be nervous and easily overwhelmed at first. Simply make sure that it has the food and water that it needs and a soft bed or crate to sleep in.

Many rescue maltipoos will gravitate towards spending time by themselves at first, and they will want a lot of space to hide and be quiet for a while. One great thing that you can do is to set up a room for your rescue maltipoo and simply stay in there with it. Do not try to engage your maltipoo at first. Simply sit close by quietly for a while. Play with your phone, or get some work done. Eventually, your maltipoo will come out, even if it takes a little while. It is important to allow your maltipoo to approach you on your own terms, rather than forcing your new dog to interact with you.

Keep track of what makes your maltipoo flinch. If your rescue dog has been abused by its previous owner, you will find that it may have negative reactions to a number of things. Some rescues have strong fear reactions to things like belts, raised hands, sticks or raised voices. Others may be very skittish around people with certain attributes, like larger men or women with hair of a certain length. Still others react strongly to basic command words, like "sit" or "come."

Keep track of what triggers anxiety, fear or aggression in your dog. Some things, like a certain word or certain items can be avoided, and other things will need a long acclimatization process. For example, if your maltipoo is troubled around larger males, and you have a tall son, it is best to allow your dog plenty of time to realize that your son is not a threat.

Speak soothingly to your dog. This gives it a little bit of stimulus and it gets it used to the sound of your voice. When the dog is getting a little braver, you might want to put treats down for it. You can put the treats closer and closer to where you are sitting until the maltipoo is willing to come close to you.

Once again, when the dog gets close to you, remember not to grab it. Instead, simply offer the dog your hand, palm down and low to the ground. This shows the dog that you are not going to strike it, and that the dog can take things at its own pace.

The great thing about many rescue maltipoos is that they are quite loving. They will warm up to you with time, but you must remember to be patient!

Some rescue maltipoos get along well with other dogs, and some do not. If you already have dogs in the home, it is a good idea to spend some time thinking about whether they will get along with a dog that likely cannot assert itself very well or that might be extra-aggressive. If you have a dog that is in any way aggressive, you do not want a rescue of any sort, for example!

Many rescues will allow you to bring your existing pets to meet the maltipoo, and if you can take advantage of that, do so. It is a good idea to see how the maltipoo will react to your dog and vice versa.

Some people have dogs that are very loving, and this can be a great thing if you have a nervous maltipoo. A patient and kind dog that loves to love other dogs is a good choice when you are looking at rescue animals in general.

Remember that taking on a rescue animal is something that requires an investment in time and love. While a lot of love and care can bring around almost any animal, you will find that it can take years before your rescue maltipoo calms down completely.

One of the worst things that can happen to rescue animals is to be returned to the rescue. They are a little older, they have another home situation that did not work out for them, and in some cases, they have picked up some new issues. Make sure that when you commit to a rescue animal that you commit to it for its entire life. Identification Tags are required for all dogs, no matter what their size, and you will discover that it is quite important to make sure that you get your maltipoo its first set of tags very quickly.

Dog tags are easy to buy, and you can have them made in just about any pet store that you care to name. When you go to get these tags engraved, remember that the only information on it should be your own name and your contact information.

Do not put your dog's name on the ID, as that can actually make it easier for people to steal your dog and to keep it calm as they do it!

Another thing for you to remember is that your maltipoo needs to be microchipped. A microchip is a very small electronic storage system that can be injected into your dog. It stays there for the maltipoo's entire life, and it can be updated by the veterinarian if you move. If your dog slips its collar and ends up at a veterinarian's office, they can scan it and give you a call.

It is best to make sure that your maltipoo has a bright and vivid collar that contrasts well with its fur. This ensures that your maltipoo will be easy to distinguish as a pet animal rather than as a feral. If you live in an area that has a lot of feral animals, it can make the difference between someone going to pick your maltipoo up versus someone just assuming that it is a stray.

# Chapter 6) Maltipoo Grooming

Both Malteses and poodles have above average grooming needs, and it makes sense that your maltipoo will have similar issues. Because there is a very wide variation in terms of the fur that is produced by maltipoos, you must tailor your grooming regimen accordingly. Take a moment to think about what your maltipoo needs and what you have to give it.

It will be very important to get your Maltipoo puppy used to the routine of grooming early on, so that they will not be traumatized for the rest of their life, every time grooming is necessary.

Not taking the time to regularly involve your Maltipoo puppy in grooming sessions could lead to serious, unwanted behavior that may include trauma to your dog, not to mention stress or injury to you in the form of biting and scratching, that could result in a lifetime of unhappy grooming sessions.

When you neglect regular, daily or at least a weekly at home grooming session with your puppy or dog to remove tangles and keep mats to a minimum, this will not only cost you and your canine companion, in terms of possible trauma and extended time on the grooming table, it will cost you a higher fee should you you opt to have regular clipping and grooming carried out at a professional salon.

An effective home regimen will include not just surface brushing, but also getting to all those sensitive areas easily missed around the ears and collar area, the armpit area, and the back end and tail.

Do not allow yourself to get caught in the *"my dog doesn't like it"* trap which is an excuse many owners will use to avoid regular grooming sessions.

When you allow your dog to dictate whether they will permit a grooming session, you are setting a dangerous precedent that could lead to lifetime of trauma for both you and your Maltipp.

When humans neglect daily grooming routines, many dogs develop a heightened sensitivity, especially with regard to having their legs and feet held, touched, brushed or clipped and will do anything they can to avoid the process when you need to groom them.

Make a pact with yourself right from the first day you bring your puppy home, never to neglect a regular grooming routine and not to avoid sensitive areas, such as trimming toenails, just because your dog may not particular *"like"* it.

## 1) The Basics

No matter the type of fur produced by your dog, it is always best to brush your maltipoo on a regular basis. When your maltipoo is a puppy, make sure that you sit quietly with it and allow it to sniff your hands and the grooming tools that you are going to use on it. As your puppy sniffs the equipment, praise it and teach it to associate love and care with these instruments. Slowly, start grooming your puppy, and as it grows, you will have an animal that is much more laid back about allowing you to touch it and groom it.

When you are looking at daily grooming, you will find that a pin brush or a slicker brush is a good choice. These brushes are designed for dogs with different hair textures. Sweep the brush through the dog's coat, being careful to comb through the fur and remove any mats.

If you have a dog with rather fine hair, which occurs when the Maltese genetic history is stronger, consider spraying the dog's coat down with some detangling product first. Look in your local pet stores for a spray that is safe to use on dogs; do not use a spray that is meant for people.

If you run into a mat, spray it thoroughly with detangling spray, which will make it easier to work out. Then, using a special mat brush, tease at the edge of the mat carefully. By working slowly and patiently, you will discover that you can work out the vast majority of mats.

In some cases, you will need to cut the mat out. When a mat is very large and very stubborn, you may find that it is far less trouble to use a set of sharp shears to remove it. Be very careful when cutting a mat out of a dog's coat. A dog's skin is very thin and tender, and even a light snip can draw blood.

When you want to cut a mat out of your dog's fur, sandwich the mat between your forefinger and your middle finger, pushing your fingers as close as they can go to the dog's side while separating out the mat. You are using your fingers to shield your dog's skin from the shears.

Using the shears, snip carefully at the mat, dividing it up into successively smaller mats. As the mats get smaller, there is a greater chance that you will be able to work them loose. This can remove mats without leaving a large gap in your dog's fur.

Check your maltipoo's ears at least once a week. Dogs get earwax buildup just like humans do, and as a breed descended from two drop-eared breeds, your maltipoo may have more problems than most. Start handling your dog's ears gently and on a regular basis to make sure that it will not resist you as it gets older.

Flip up your maltipoo's ears to look for signs of infection or for any debris. Because most maltipoos have long, floppy ears, there is a lot of opportunity for infections or illness to occur. Look for any debris, like grass seeds or dust, and use a clean rage dipped in warm water to clear out any of the earwax.

Use the corner of a cloth soaked in warm water to clean your dog's ears. If you see any redness, blood or irritation, do your best to clean it up. A small cut can often be tended to at home if it is healing well on its own.

On the other hand, a small cut can signify a big problem, especially if there is some swelling or heat in the area. Similarly, you will discover that a strong odor can signify signs of infection. If you detect these signs, you should take your maltipoo to the veterinarian.

## 2) Bathing

There are a few different schools of thought when it comes to bathing a maltipoo. Some people prefer to leave it to the pros, and thus end up bathing their dog every month or so. Other people feel that maltipoos benefit from being bathed every week or every other week.

Before you get your Maltipoo anywhere near the water, it's important to make sure that you brush out any debris, knots or tangles from their coat before you begin the bathing process because getting knots or tangles wet could make them tighter and much more difficult to remove, which will cause your dog pain and distress.

As well, removing any debris from your dog's coat beforehand, including dead undercoat and shedding hair will make the entire process easier on both you, your dog, and your drains, which will become clogged with hair if you don't remove it beforehand.

**TIP**: no dog likes to have water poured over it's head and into it's eyes, so use a wet sponge or wash cloth to wet the head area.

The variation in opinion likely stems from the fact that there are a lot of different dogs called maltipoos, and at the end of the day, you simply need to make the decision that works best for you and your dog. Bathe your dog when its fur looks a little dull or limp, or bathe it when its fur has a bit of an odor.

You can start bathing a maltipoo within a few weeks of weaning it, but if the house is a little cold, the dog is under the weather or if you are still trying to win the puppy's trust, it is fine to leave off this task for a short time.

To bathe your maltipoo, start by filling up your bathroom or kitchen sink with about 3 inches or 7.62 centimeters of warm water. Set your maltipoo into the water gently and allow it to get comfortable. Do not allow it to jump out.

Use your hand or a small cup to pour water over the dog's back, wetting its fur thoroughly. Unless your dog is very docile, skip washing the fur on its head until you are more comfortable with each other.

After the dog's fur is entirely wet, massage in a very small amount of hypoallergenic dog shampoo. Do not use human shampoo, and do not use one of the standard dog brands. Maltipoos tend to have relatively delicate skin, and the result is that you must always be careful about the shampoo that you are using.

Rinse the shampoo out completely, and apply a small amount of hypoallergenic conditioner to the dog's fur, following the written instructions. Some treatments need to sit for a bit, while others can be rinsed out quickly.

Rinse out the dog's fur, making sure that you get every speck of shampoo and conditioner. Dogs can occasionally make themselves sick by licking themselves after they have been bathed, so be careful.

After the bath, be sure that your maltipoo is completely dried before you allow it to scamper off and play. A dog that is a bit on the delicate side can catch a cold very quickly, and even a hardy dog can run straight to the nearest dusty corner and roll, undoing all of your hard work!

When you want to dry a wet maltipoo, the most efficient way to do so is to use a hairdryer turned to low. To make sure that all of the dog's fur is getting dried, use a straight comb to lift up the dog's fur, allowing you to dry the underside. Some maltipoos have relatively coarse hair that does not mat easily, and if your dog has a coat like that, you can gently scrub a dry towel over the dog's fur to dry it. On the other hand, if your dog has soft silky fur, this can lead to tangles. Use your best judgment when you are looking to keep your dog fresh and clean.

## 3) Professional Grooming

Maltipoos are dogs with ancestry that includes two breeds with fur that requires very specialized care. Poodle fur has more in common with human hair than most dog fur, and Maltese fur is known for being very slick, sleek and fine.

With all of that in mind, it should come as no surprise that your maltipoo will have different requirements when it comes to good grooming. When your maltipoo puppy is about four months old, it is time for its first visit to the groomer. Before this point, puppies just do not have the attention span to sit down and have their fur clipped, no matter how skilled the person doing the clipping is.

Your groomer will take a good look at your puppy and tell you what you need to do with it and the schedule on which you need to bring your dog in. While some people dismiss grooming as a solely cosmetic procedure, good grooming is actually an important health task for dogs with longer coats.

Dogs that are not well groomed will pick up mats, and the skin underneath those mats can grow to be red and inflamed. If you want to make sure that your maltipoo stays in good health, regular grooming is an essential part of how you should proceed.

A good groomer will take care of several tasks for you. They will keep your dog clipped and comfortable, they will trim the dog's toenails if they need it, and they will express the dog's anal glands if necessary. These are all tasks that are handled quickly and competently, though there may or may not be an extra charge attached.

When you are invested in making sure that your maltipoo looks great, discuss different cuts with the groomer. There is no standard clip for the maltipoo, but one short cut that is fairly easy to maintain is the puppy cut, where all of the fur on the body is cut short while the fur on the head and the feet are left longer.

Before you choose a specific cut for your maltipoo, remember to ask what it takes to maintain it and how often you need to see the groomer.

Though it might be tempting to save on the cost, you need to remember that grooming dogs is a skilled position. It requires time and effort, and if you do it yourself, you risk giving your dog a foolish style at the very least, and at the very worst, you may even injure it. Grooming a moving, living animal is a lot different from cutting a dummy's hair or even your own hair, so leave the vast majority of the complicated grooming tasks to your groomer.

An average price for professionally grooming a small Maltipoo will usually start around $40 (£24) and could be considerably more depending upon whether the salon is also bathing and trimming nails.

## 4) Clipping

If you have decided to learn how to clip your Maltipoo's hair yourself, rather than taking them to a professional grooming salon, you will need to purchase all the tools necessary and learn how to properly use them.

The first step will be learning which blades to use in your electric clipper in order to get the length of cut you desire.

The "blade cut" refers to the length of the dog's hair that will remain after cutting against the natural line of the hair.

As an example, if the blade cut indicates 1/4" (0.6 cm), the length of your Maltipoo's hair after cutting will be 1/4" (0.6 cm) if you cut with the natural growth of their hair, or it will be 1/8" (0.3 cm) if you cut against the direction of the hair growth.

Even if you decide to leave the full grooming to the professionals, in between grooming sessions you will still need to have a brush, a comb, a small pair of scissors and a pair of nail clippers on hand, so that you can keep the hair clipped away from your Maltipoo's eyes, knots and tangles out of their coat and their nails trimmed short.

A good quality clipper for a Maltipoo, such as an *"Andis"*, *"Wahl"* or *"Oster"* professional electric clipper will cost between $100 and $300 (£60 and £180) or more.

## 5) Nail Care

### a) Nail clipping

Maltipoo toenails are just like human nails in that they are always growing and they sometimes need to be cut. The rate at which your dog needs his nails cut is something that varies from dog to dog. A maltipoo that goes on a lot of walks on the city pavement will wear down its nails a lot faster than a dog that spends all of its time playing in parks, but both dogs will need their nails cut eventually.

When you are looking at cutting your dog's nails, you might choose to have a groomer do it, or you might choose to do it yourself.

To cut your dog's nails, you need a pair of nail trimmers designed for dogs and a small container of cornstarch.

Calm your dog down and hold one of its feet in one hand. Examine its nails closely. Like humans, dogs have a nail bed, known as the quick, which will bleed if you cut it. On white dogs or dogs that are lighter in color, you can see the quick easily as a line of pink underneath the dog's claw. It is harder to see in black dogs and dogs that are darker in color.

What you want to do is to cut the nail about 2 millimeters above the quick. Work fast, and use the clippers according to their instructions. When you are using the scissor-style clippers, you will find that you need to hold the clippers perpendicular to the claw, not directly along it the way you would for a person.

Work fast, and do not be surprised if your dog tries to twist away. If you accidentally cut your dog's quick, be prepared for a yelp, some blood and some pain. If this occurs, push the dog's bleeding cut into the tub of cornstarch, which will stop the bleeding right away.

Do not be surprised if your dog does not allow you to cut more than one paw at a time. While there are some very laid back dogs that do not mind having their nails cut, the vast majority of them will protest a fair amount.

If you have a puppy, you can train them to be more easy-going about having their feet touched or played with. When the puppy is still small, pick up one of its feet while speaking to it soothingly. Over time, you will find that the puppy cares less and less that you are holding its feet.

## b) Nail care

If you love the look of a well-groomed dog, your attention to your maltipoo's nails might go beyond merely cutting them! Many dog owners decide that their dogs would benefit from a coat of nail polish, but before you go ahead, there are a few things to keep in mind.

Firstly, remember that human nail polish contains materials that are quite toxic if they are ingested. Then remember how curious maltipoos are and how likely they are to want to lick things that they do not understand.

There are people out there who have put human nail polish on their dogs and had no ill effects, but when it comes to a dog as vulnerable and small as a maltipoo, it is better to be safe than sorry!

Use a nail polish that is meant for dogs, and before you apply it, check your dog's paws. Make sure that there are no cracks and no cuts, as both the polish and the remover can aggravate the dog's skin.

Watch your dog carefully when you start to apply the nail polish and after. If you see that your maltipoo is constantly chewing at the nail polish, there is a chance that it will end up with an upset stomach no matter what you do. Similarly, chewing at nails can be seen as a sign of stress.

Painting your maltipoo's nails is quite a cute look, but remember that you should not sacrifice your dog's health for aesthetics.

During the winter, some people do apply coconut oil to their maltipoo's nails to keep them strong and to prevent cracking, but remember to use just a very small amount.

Allowing your Maltipoo to have long, untrimmed nails can result in various health hazards including infections or an irregular and uncomfortable gait that can result in damage to their skeleton.

Although most dogs do not particularly enjoy the process of having their nails trimmed, and most humans find the exercise to be a little scary, regular nail trimming is a very important grooming practice that should never be overlooked.

In order to keep your Maltipoo's toenails in good condition and the proper length, you will need to purchase either a guillotine or plier nail trimmer at a pet store and learn how to correctly use it.

**NOTE**: when your Maltipoo is a small puppy, it will be best to trim their nails with a pair of nail scissors, which you can purchase at any pet store, that are smaller and easier to use on smaller nails.

Furthermore, if you want your dog's nails to be smooth, without the sharp edges clipping alone can create, you will also want to invest in a toenail file or a special, slow speed, rotary trimmer (Dremel™), designed especially for dog nails. Some dogs will prefer the rotary trimmer to the squeezing sensation of the nail clipper.

**NOTE**: <u>never</u> use a regular Dremel™ tool on a dog's toenails as it will be too high speed and will burn your dog's toenails. Only use a slow speed Dremel™, Model 7300-PT Pet Nail Grooming Tool.

## 6) Maltipoo Fur Type

Maltipoos may take after their poodle parent, their Maltese parent or simply be a mixture of the two when it comes to their fur type. There is no standard when it comes to maltipoo fur, so you may end up with a maltipoo puppy that has any one of the three types. Make sure that you have an idea of which fur type your maltipoo has and what kind of care it receives. Maltipoos that take a great deal after their Maltese parent have fur that is rather straight, fine and silky. This coat tends to be fairly slippery, and as a result, it will not tangle very much at all. Sometimes this fur is very thick, meaning that it can be a little unruly across the board. If you have a maltipoo with a rather silky, straight coat, make sure that you get it professionally groomed every four to six weeks. This is how you keep this coat looking soft, shiny and lustrous.

Maltipoos can also have coats that are virtually identical to the coats of their poodle parent, meaning that their fur is going to be very dense and curly. This fur has a few qualities that give it more in common with human hair than with the fur of other dogs, and because of this, some specialized care is needed. This type of fur needs to be groomed regularly, though how regularly depends on the cut that you have chosen. If you want something rather sculptured, be prepared to go in every four to five weeks. On the other hand, if you prefer something that is a lot shorter and clean, like a puppy cut, schedule grooming for every eight to ten weeks.

The most rare type of coat found in maltipoos is also the most difficult to deal with, and that is the style that mixes the poodle and Maltese heritages. Instead of being curly, this fur is wavy, and instead of being fine, it's rather wiry and stiff. This type of fur is rather inclined towards matting, and that means that you should be very careful with it. A fair amount of regular work is usually required to make this coat look good, even if it is simply running a brush through it on a regular basis. This is definitely a coat type that requires conditioner when you bathe the dog, and it is best if you take this dog to the groomer every month or so.

When you are looking to make sure that your maltipoo looks great, pay close attention to the kind of fur that it has. Sleeker coats require more careful efforts when it comes to detangling, but denser coats will mat up more often. Learning about your maltipoo's hairstyle is something that can make a huge difference when you are trying to keep it in good shape.

## 7) Ear Care

There are many ear cleaning creams, drops, oils, rinses, solutions and wipes formulated for cleaning your dog's ears that you can purchase from your local pet store or veterinarian's office.

Or you may prefer to use a home remedy that will just as efficiently clean your Maltipoo's ears, such as Witch Hazel or a 50:50 mixture of hydrogen peroxide and purified water.

**Tip**: if you are going to make your own ear cleaning solution, find a bottle with a nozzle, measure your solution, properly diluted and mixed into the bottle, and use your preparation to saturate a cloth to wipe out the visible part of your dog's ears. Always make sure that the ears are totally dried after cleaning.

## 8) Eye Care

Although some breeds, like the Maltipoo, are much more prone to build up of daily eye secretions, every dog should have their eyes regularly wiped with a warm, damp cloth to remove build up of daily secretions in the corners of the eyes.

The Maltipoo will be prone to a build up of secretions that can be unattractive and uncomfortable for the dog as the hair becomes glued together.

If this build up is not removed every day it can quickly become a cause of bacterial yeast growth that can lead to eye infections.

When you take a moment every day to gently wipe your dog's eyes with a warm, moist cloth, and keep the hair trimmed away from their eyes, you will help to keep your dog's eyes comfortable and infection free.

## 9) Dental Care

As a conscientious Maltipoo guardian you will need to regularly care for your dog's teeth throughout their entire life.

## a) Retained Primary Teeth

Often a young dog will not naturally lose their puppy or baby teeth, especially those with small jaws, like the Maltipoo, without intervention from a licensed veterinarian.

Therefore, keep a close watch on your puppy's teeth around the age of 6 or 7 months of age to make certain that the baby teeth have fallen out and that the adult teeth have space to grown in.

If your Maltipoo puppy has not naturally lost their baby teeth, they will need to be pulled, in order to allow room for the adult teeth to grow in, and the best time to do this will be at the same time they visit the veterinarian's office to be spayed or neutered.

Smaller dogs, like the Maltipoo, have a smaller jaw, which can result in more problems with teeth overcrowding.

An overcrowded mouth can cause teeth to grow unevenly or crooked and food and plaque to build up, which will eventually result in bacterial growth on the surface of the teeth, causing bad breath, gum and dental disease.

## b) Periodontal Disease

Please be aware that 80% of three-year-old dogs suffer from periodontal disease and bad breath because their guardians do not look after their dog's teeth.

What makes this shocking statistic even worse is that it is entirely possible to prevent canine gum disease and bad breath.

The pain associated with periodontal disease will make your dog's life miserable, as it will be painful for them to eat and the associated bacteria can infect many parts of the dog's body, including the heart, kidney, liver and brain, and they will have to suffer in silence.

If your Maltipoo has bad breath, this could be the first sign of gum disease caused by plaque build-up on the teeth.

In addition, if your Maltipoo is drooling excessively, this may be a secondary symptom to dental disease. Your dog may be experiencing pain or the salivary glands may be reacting to inflammation from excessive bacteria in the mouth. If you notice your Maltipoo drooling, you will want to have them professionally examined at your veterinarian's office.

## c) Teeth Brushing

Slowly introduce your Maltipoo to teeth brushing early on in their young life so that they will not fear it.

Maltipoos, particularly rescue maltipoos, can have issues with their teeth. Like most dogs, when their teeth are not cared for, they can rot and lead to serious problems down the line. When you bring your maltipoo puppy home, you will discover that it is quite important to make sure that you get it used to tooth brushing, which can prevent dental issues in dogs just as it prevents dental issues in humans.

When you are picking up supplies for tooth brushing, do not simply default to what you get for yourself at the grocery store. Go to the pet store, and choose a toothbrush and toothpaste for a dog. It may be a bit before you can use them on your puppy, but it is better to have them to hand than not.

Sit your maltipoo puppy on your lap and give it the command that it will associate with tooth brushing, like "teeth" or "mouth." While holding the puppy securely, slide your finger along your puppy's mouth and gums gently but firmly. Praise your puppy when it can sit through the process without squirming.

Once your puppy is comfortable with you putting your fingers in its mouth, it is time to introduce it to the toothbrush. Start by simply showing your puppy the toothbrush and allowing it to sniff at the brush and to get to know it.

When the puppy is comfortable with the toothbrush, insert the brush into the puppy's mouth just the way that you would your finger. Leave it still at first, but as your puppy gets more comfortable with it, start moving it until you are actually brushing your puppy's teeth.

Finally, add a small amount of toothpaste to the brush. Toothpaste for dogs typically has a meaty taste that the dog will enjoy, and it does not need to be rinsed out.

**TIP**: if you need help keeping your dog's mouth open while you do a quick brush or scrape, get yourself a piece of hard material (rubber or leather) that they can bite down on, so that they cannot fully close their mouth while you work on their teeth.

When using an electric toothbrush, they will get used to the buzzing of the electric brush, which will do a superior job of cleaning their teeth.

Firstly, let them see the electric brush, then let them hear it buzzing, and before you put it in their mouth, let them feel the buzzing sensation on their body, while you move it slowly toward their head and muzzle.

When your Maltipoo will allow you to touch their muzzle while the brush is turned on, the next step is to brush a couple of teeth at a time until they get used to having them all brushed at the same time.

Whether you let the electric toothbrush do the work for you, or you are using a manual toothbrush, make sure that you brush in a circular motion with the bristles of the brush angled so that they get underneath the gum line to help prevent gum disease and loose teeth.

Make sure that you brush your dog's teeth every day or every few days. While you do this, you can also examine your dog's mouth for any issues, like whitish gums, bleeding gums, loose teeth or sores. This is a good way to stay up to date on your dog's health.

Another way to make sure that your dog's teeth stay healthy is to make sure that it gets regular feedings with dry kibble. Dry kibble is tougher and requires more chewing, which keeps your dog's teeth and gums healthy. On top of that, kibble will also scrape off some of the plaque that can develop on your dog's teeth.

## d) Teeth Scaling

Also, it's a good idea to get your dog used to the idea of occasionally having their teeth scraped or scaled, especially the back molars which tend to build up plaque. Be very careful if you are doing this yourself because the tools are sharp.

Use of a tooth scraper once or twice a month can help to remove plaque buildup. Most accumulation will be found on the outside of the teeth and on the back molars, near the gum line. Go slowly and carefully because these tools are sharp and only do this when your dog is calm and relaxed, a little bit at a time.

Some people choose to scrape their dog's teeth at home, but in general, this is a good task to leave for the veterinarian or a groomer.

## e) Healthy Teeth Tips

Despite what most dog owners might put up with as normal, it is <u>not</u> normal for your dog to have smelly dog breath or canine halitosis.

Bad breath is the first sign of an unhealthy mouth, which could involve gum disease or tooth decay.

The following tips will help keep your Maltipoo's mouth and teeth healthy:

- Keep your dog's teeth sparkling white and their breath fresh by using old-fashioned hydrogen as your doggy toothpaste (hydrogen peroxide is what's in the human whitening toothpaste). There will be such a small amount on the brush that it will not harm your dog, and will kill any bacteria in your dog's mouth.

- Many canine toothpastes are formulated with active enzymes to help keep tartar build-up at bay.

- Help prevent tooth plaque and doggy halitosis by feeding your dog natural, hard bones at least once a month, which will also help to remove tartar while polishing and keeping their teeth white. Feed large bones so there is no danger of swallowing, and do NOT boil the bones first because this makes the bone soft (which defeats the purpose of removing plaque), and could cause it to splinter into smaller pieces that could create a choking hazard for your dog.

- Small dogs with shorter muzzles such as the Maltipoo tend to be more vulnerable to teeth and gum problems, therefore, you really need to be brushing their teeth every single day.

- Feed a daily dental chew or hard biscuit to help to remove tartar while exercising jaws and massaging gums. Some dental chews contain natural breath freshening cinnamon, cloves or chlorophyll.

- Coconut oil also helps to prevent smelly dog breath while giving your dog's digestive, immune and metabolic functions a boost at the same time. Dogs love the taste, so add a 1/2 tsp to your Maltipoo's dinner and their breath will soon be much sweeter.

## 10) Skin Care

Keeping your Maltipoo's coat clean by regularly bathing with canine shampoo and conditioner and free from debris and parasites, as well as providing plenty of clean water and feeding them a high quality diet free from allergy-causing ingredients will go a long way toward keeping their skin healthy and itch-free.

## 11) Brushing and Combing

Brushing and combing your dog's coat is an often-overlooked task that is a necessary part of maintaining your dog's health.

In addition, taking time to brush and comb your Maltipoo's coat will also give you an opportunity to bond with your dog, while identifying any problems early on (such as lumps or bumps and matted hair), before they may become more serious.

Make sure that your grooming sessions are as pleasant as possible by choosing the right tools for a Maltipoo and their type and length of coat.

You will need a variety of brushes and combs to keep your Maltipoo's coat in good condition that will include a soft bristle brush, a slicker brush and a pin brush.

As well as your collection of brushes, you will need to invest in a metal comb, a flea comb and perhaps a mat splitter.

## 12) Bleaching

Though maltipoos can come in any color, the color that most people think about when it comes to this lovely breed is white. Malteses are all white, and poodles often are too.

When maltipoos are young puppies, they are quite lovely and white, but that is generally because they are not allowed outside very much! If you want to make sure that your maltipoo stays sparkling white, there are a few things to keep in mind.

Firstly, make sure that you use a whitening shampoo on your maltipoo's fur. A whitening shampoo works the way that shampoo for older people going gray does. It helps improve the shine and it reduces the gray by adding a very small amount of bleaching agent to the mix.

Do not use bleaching solutions that are designed to sit in your dog's fur. These are often very powerful solutions, and they can actually hurt your dog's fur if you leave them in too long. Remember that maltipoos have very delicate skin and that they are very vulnerable in this way.

Whenever your maltipoo goes outside, use a damp, warm cloth to clean it up as soon as it comes inside. Remember that allowing dirt and mud to sit on your dog's fur is something that can cause staining after an extended period of time.

In general, if you are worried about your maltipoo's coat, simply keep track of where it goes. If you want to keep your maltipoo's fur white, you may be better off going to an indoor dog park than you would allowing your dog to roam around your yard.

## 13) Equipment & Supplies Required

A **bristle brush** with its clusters of tightly-packed bristles will remove loose hair, dirt and debris while gently stimulating the skin, improving circulation and adding shine to the coat.

A **pin brush** usually has an oval head with wire bristles that are individually spaced and embedded into a flexible rubber pad.

Most guardians prefer pin brushes with rubber tips as these help to prevent a wire from accidentally piercing a dog's sensitive skin.

A pin brush is more normally used following a thorough bristle brushing to lift and fluff the hair at the end of a grooming session.

A **slicker brush** has short, thin, wire bristles arranged closely together and anchored to a flat, often rectangular, surface that's attached to a handle.

A slicker brush is an ideal grooming tool for helping to remove mats and tangles from a Maltipoo's coat. Slicker brushes are often used as a finishing brush after the use of a pin brush to smooth the dog's coat and create a shiny finish.

**Mat Splitters,** as the name suggests, are tools for splitting apart matted hair, and they come in three different types, including the letter opener style, the safety razor style and the curved blade style.

All of these tools are used to split matted fur into smaller, lengthwise pieces, with minimal discomfort to the dog, so that you or your groomer can untangle or shave the area with a clipper.

**Combs** are very useful for getting down to the base of any tangles in a dog's coat and working them loose before they develop into painful mats.

Most metal combs have a combination of widely spaced and narrow spaced teeth and are designed so that if you run into a tangle, you can switch to the wider spaced teeth while you work it out, without pulling and irritating your dog.

**NOTE**: Some combs have rotating teeth which makes the process of removing tangles from your Maltipoo's coat much easier on them without the pain of pulling and snagging.

**Flea combs**, as the name suggests, are designed for the specific purpose of removing fleas from a dog's coat.

A flea comb is usually small in size for maneuvering in tight spaces, and may be made of plastic or metal with the teeth of the comb placed very close together, to trap hiding fleas.

As well, you will want to keep a good quality pair of small **scissors** in your Maltipoo grooming box, even if you do not want to do the full grooming process yourself, so that you can regularly trim around your Maltipoo's eyes between full grooming sessions.

If you are planning to groom your Maltipoo yourself, you will need to invest in good quality scissors of several lengths that can cost anywhere between $30 and $200 each (£18 and £119) or more.

## 14) The Older Maltipoo

There are several issues that older maltipoos face that should be considered as part of their care.

The biggest one to think about is the fact that, like many small dogs, their joints will deteriorate as they age. The key to caring for a small dog that has failing joints involves helping it put as little pressure on those joints as possible. Instead of allowing your dog to jump up on the bed, for example, give it a ramp. Carry your maltipoo up stairs or build a ramp over the stairs for the dog.

Some maltipoos also have reduced vision as they age, and there are a few solutions for this as well. First and foremost, make sure that the layout of your home stays consistent. Moving landmarks can confuse your dog or disorient it to the point where it runs into walls. Leaving your furniture in one place and making sure most doors stay open prevent injuries.

As a dog's mobility and balance gets worse, start taking precautions like watching your dog when it gets near the stairs or installing baby gates.

Some older maltipoos, depending on the condition of their bodies, also become incontinent as they age. At this point, either carry your dog outside or consider the purchase of puppy pads again.

Remember that you should always consider your maltipoo's happiness and quality of life. What can you do to make it more comfortable? Pay attention to any sounds that it is making, and always make sure that you see what your dog wants to do and whether it is having troubles.

## 15) Grooming Products

### a) Shampoos

NEVER make the mistake of using human shampoo or conditioner for bathing your Maltipoo because dogs have a different pH balance than humans.

For example, shampoo for humans has a pH balance of 5.5, whereas shampoo formulated for our canine companions has an almost neutral pH balance of 7.5.

Any shampoo with a lower pH balance will be harmful to your dog because it will be too harshly acidic for their coat and skin, which can create skin problems.

Always purchase a shampoo for your dog that is specially formulated to be gentle and moisturizing on your Maltipoo's coat and skin, that will not strip the natural oils, and which will nourish your dog's coat to give it a healthy shine.

As a general rule, always read the instructions provided on the shampoo bottle, and avoid shampoos containing insecticides or harsh chemicals.

**Tip**: if your Maltipoo is suffering from an infestation of fleas, you may want to bathe them with shampoo containing pyrethrum (a botanical extract found in small, white daisies) or a shampoo containing citrus oil.

## b) Conditioners

While many of us humans use a conditioner after we shampoo our own hair, a large number of us canine guardians forget to use a conditioner on our own dog's coat after bathing.

Even if the bathing process is one that you wish to complete as quickly as possible, you will want to reconsider this; just as conditioning our human hair improves its condition, the same is true for our dog's coat.

Conditioning your Maltipoo's coat will not only make it look and feel better, but will also add additional benefits, including:

- Preventing the escape of natural oils and moisture;
- Keeping the coat cleaner for a longer period of time;
- Repairing a coat that has become damaged or dry;
- Restoring a soft, silky feel;
- A conditioned coat will dry more quickly;
- Protection from the heat of the dryer and breakage from tangles during toweling, combing or brushing.

Spend the extra two minutes to condition your Maltipoo's coat after bathing because the benefits of doing so will be appreciated by both you and your dog, which will have an overall healthy coat and skin with a natural shine.

## c) De-tanglers

There are many de-tangling products you can purchase which will make the job of combing and removing mats much easier on both you and your Maltipoo, especially if you have opted to let their hair grow longer.

De-tangling products work by making the hair slippery, and while some de-tanglers work well when used full strength, you may prefer a lighter, spray-in product.

As well, there are silicone products and grooming powders, or you can even use cornstarch to effectively lubricate the hair to help with removing mats and tangles before bathing.

## d) Styptic Powder

You will always want to avoid causing any pain when trimming your Maltipoo's toenails, because you don't want to destroy their trust in you regularly performing this task.

However, accidents do happen, therefore if you accidentally cut into the vein in the toenail, know that you will cause your dog pain, and the toenail will bleed.

Therefore, it is always a good idea to keep some styptic powder (often called "Kwik Stop") in your grooming kit. Dip a moistened finger into the powder and apply it immediately to the end of the bleeding nail.

The quickest way to stop a nail from bleeding is to immediately apply styptic powder and firm pressure for a few seconds.

**Tip**: if you do not have styptic powder or a styptic pencil available, there are several home remedies that can help stop the bleeding, including a mixture of baking soda and cornstarch, or simply cornstarch alone. Also, a cold, wet teabag or rubbing with scent-free soap can also be effective. These home remedies will not be as instantly effective as styptic powder.

## e) Ear Powders

Ear powders, which can be purchased at any pet store, are designed to help keep your dog's ears dry while at the same time inhibiting the growth of bacteria that can lead to infections.

## f) Ear Cleaning Solutions

Your local pet store will offer a wide variety of ear cleaning creams, drops, oils, rinses, solutions and wipes specially formulated for cleaning your dog's ears.

There are also many home remedies that will just as efficiently clean your dog's ears.

**Note**: because a dog's ears are a very sensitive area, always read the labels before purchasing products and avoid any solutions that list alcohol as the main ingredient.

## g) Home Ear Cleaning Solutions

The following are three effective home solutions that will efficiently clean your dog's ears:

**Witch Hazel** is a natural anti-inflammatory that works well to cleanse and protect against infection while encouraging faster healing of minor skin traumas.

A 50:50 solution of **Organic Apple Cider Vinegar and Purified Water** has been used as an external folk medicine for decades. This mixture is a gentle and effective solution that kills germs while naturally healing.

A 50:50 solution of **Hydrogen Peroxide and Purified Water** is useful for cleansing wounds and dissolving earwax.

Whatever product you decide to use for cleaning your dog's ears, always be careful about what you put into your dog's ears and thoroughly dry them after cleaning.

### h) Canine Toothpastes

When it comes time to brush a dog's teeth, this is where many guardians fail miserably, using the excuse that *"my dog doesn't like it"*. Whether they like it or not is not the issue, because in order to keep your Maltipoo healthy, they must have healthy teeth and the only way to ensure this is to brush their teeth every day.

The many canine toothpastes on the market are usually flavored with beef or chicken in an attempt to appeal to the dog's taste buds, while others may be infused with mint or some other breath freshening ingredient in an attempt to appeal to humans by improving the dog's breath.

Honestly, your dog is not going to be begging for you to brush his or her teeth no matter how tasty the paste might be, therefore, effectiveness, in the shortest period of time, will be more of a deciding factor than whether or not your dog prefers the taste of the toothpaste.

Some dog toothpastes contain baking soda, which is the same mild abrasive found in many human pastes, and it is designed to gently scrub the teeth. However, just how much time you will have to spend scrubbing your dog's teeth, before they've had enough, may be too minimal to make these pastes very effective.

Other types of canine toothpastes are formulated with enzymes that are designed to work chemically by breaking down tartar or plaque in the dog's mouth. These pastes do not need to be washed off your dog's teeth and are safe for them to swallow. Whether or not they remain on the dog's teeth long enough to do any good might be debatable.

**Tip**: old-fashioned hydrogen peroxide cleans while killing germs and keeping teeth white. Just dip your dog's toothbrush in a capful of hydrogen peroxide, shake off the excess, and brush their teeth. There will be such a small amount in your dog's mouth that you don't need to worry about them swallowing it.

## i) Paw Creams

Depending upon the types of surfaces our canine counterparts usually walk on, they may suffer from cracked or rough pads.

You can restore resiliency and keep your Maltipoo's paws in healthy condition by regularly applying a cream or lotion to protect their paw pads.

**TIP**:  a good time to do this is just after you have clipped their nails.

# Chapter 7) Training a Maltipoo

Maltipoos are wonderful dogs, but one issue that they face is that they have a reputation for being ill-tempered spoiled brats! The truth of the matter lies not in this dog breed's temperament, but rather in the fact that their owners do not train them.

As is evident, maltipoos do not get very large. Unlike huskies, pit bulls and Rottweilers, they are not perceived as dangerous. Because of this, owners do not feel the need to train them, and this can lead to issues that are not only irritating but dangerous.

Remember that any dog can deliver a bite that is dangerous to a human and will require stitches. Any dog can pull away from its owner and run into a crowd or into the street.

When you train your maltipoo, you are ensuring its safety and the safety of everyone around you.

## 1) House Training

### a) Human Training

House training, or "potty" training, is a critical first step in the education of any new puppy, and the first part of a successful process is training the human guardian.

When you bring home your new Maltipoo puppy, they will be relying upon your guidance to teach them what they need to learn. Maltipoos are known to be relatively quick learners, and barring the odd accident, they do very well.
Remember that a young puppy only does not have full control over its bladder yet.

When you provide your puppy with your consistent patience and understanding, they are capable of learning rules at a very early age, and house training is no different, especially since it's all about establishing a regular routine.

Potty training a new puppy takes time and patience — how much time depends entirely upon you.

Check in with yourself and make sure your energy remains consistently calm and patient and that you exercise plenty of compassion and understanding while you help your new puppy learn the new bathroom rules.

Maltipoo puppies and dogs flourish with routines and so do humans, therefore, the first step is to establish a daily routine that will work well for both canine and human alike.

For instance, depending upon the age of your Maltipoo puppy, make a plan to take them out for a bathroom break every two hours and stick to it because while you are in the beginning stages of potty training, the more vigilant and consistent you can be, the quicker and more successful your results will be.

Generally speaking, while your puppy is still growing, a young puppy can hold it approximately one hour for every month of their age.

The rule of thumb states that a puppy that is four months old can hold its urine for four hours, a five month old puppy can hold it for five hours and so on. When the puppy gets to be about eight or nine hours, you have reached its adult capacity.

This means that if your 2-month-old puppy has been happily snoozing for a couple of hours, as soon as they wake up, they will need to go outside.

Unless you catch your dog in the act of urinating or defecating in the house, do not punish it. The old technique of rubbing a dog's nose in its mess is abusive; it does not teach the dog to be anything but afraid of you.

Some of the first indications or signs that your puppy needs to be taken outside to relieve themselves will be when you see them:

- Sniffing around
- Circling
- Looking for the door
- Whining, crying or barking
- Acting agitated

It will be important to always take your Maltipoo puppy out first thing every morning, and immediately after they wake up from a nap as well as soon after they have finished eating a meal or having a big drink of water.

Also, your happy praise goes a long way toward encouraging and reinforcing future success when your Maltipoo puppy makes the right decisions, so let them know you are happy when they do their business in the right place.

Initially, treats can be a good way to reinforce how happy you are that your puppy is learning to relieve themselves in the right place. Slowly, treats can be removed and replaced with your happy praise.

Next, now that you have a new puppy in your life, you will want to be flexible with respect to adapting your schedule to meet the requirements that will help to quickly teach your Maltipoo puppy their new bathroom routine.

This means not leaving your puppy alone for endless hours at a time because firstly, they are pack animals that need companionship and your direction at all times, plus long periods alone will result in the disruption of the potty training schedule you have worked hard to establish.

If you have no choice but to leave your puppy alone for many hours, make sure that you place them in a paper lined room or pen where they can relieve themselves without destroying your favorite carpet.

Remember, your Maltipoo is a growing puppy with a bladder and bowels that they do not yet have complete control over and you will have a much happier time and better success if you simply train yourself to pay attention to when your young companion is showing signs of needing to relieve themselves.

## b) Bell Training

A very easy way to introduce your new Maltipoo puppy to house training is to begin by teaching them how to ring a doorbell whenever they need to go outside.

Ringing a doorbell is not only a convenient alert system for both you and your Maltipoo puppy or dog, your visitors will be most impressed by how smart your Maltipoo is.

A further benefit of training your puppy to ring a bell is that you will not have to listen to your puppy or dog whining, barking or howling to be let out, and your door will not become scratched up from their nails.

Unless you prefer to purchase an already manufactured doggy doorbell or system, take a trip to your local novelty store and purchase a small bell that has a nice, loud ring.

Attach the bell to a piece of ribbon or string and hang it from a door handle or tape it to a windowsill near the door where you will be taking your puppy out when they need to relieve themselves. The string will need to be long enough so that your Maltipoo puppy can easily reach the bell with their nose or a paw.

Next, each time you take your puppy out to relieve itself, say the word *"Out"*, and use their paw or their nose to ring the bell. Praise them for this "trick" and immediately take them outside.

The only down side to teaching your Maltipoo puppy or dog to ring a bell when they want to go outside is that even if they don't actually have to go out to relieve themselves, but just want to go outside because they are bored, you will still have to take them out every time they ring the bell.

There are many types and styles of *"gotta' go"* commercially manufactured bells you could choose, ranging from the elegant **"Poochie Bells™"** that hang from a doorknob, the simple **"Tell Bell™"** that sits on the floor, or various high-tech door chime systems that function much like a doggy intercom system where they push a pad with their paw and it rings a bell.

Whatever doorbell system you choose for your Maltipoo puppy, once they are trained, this type of an alert system is an easy way to eliminate accidents in the home.

### c) Kennel Training

Kennel training is always a good idea for any puppy early in their education, because it can be utilized for many different situations, including being a very helpful tool for house training.

When purchasing a kennel for your Maltipoo puppy, always buy a kennel that will be the correct size for your Maltipoo puppy once they become adult size. The kennel will be the correct size if your full-grown Maltipoo dog can stand up and easily turn around inside their kennel.

When you train your Maltipoo puppy to accept sleeping in their own kennel at nighttime, this will also help to accelerate their potty training, because no puppy or dog wants to relieve themselves where they sleep, which means that they will hold their bladder and bowels as long as they possibly can.

Always be kind and compassionate and remember that a puppy will be able to hold it approximately one hour for every month of their age.

Generally, a Maltipoo puppy that is three months old will be able to hold it for approximately three hours, unless they just ate a meal or had a big drink of water.

Be watchful and consistent so that you learn your Maltipoo puppy's body language, and when it's time for them to go outside. Presenting them with familiar scents, by taking them to the same spot in the yard or the same street corner will help to remind and encourage them that they are outside to relieve themselves.

Use a voice cue to remind your puppy why they are outside, such as *"go pee"* and always remember to praise them every time they relieve themselves in the right place so that they quickly understand what you expect of them and will learn to "go" on cue.

## d) Exercise Pen Training

The exercise pen is a transition from kennel only training and will be helpful for those times when you may have to leave your Maltipoo puppy for more hours than they can reasonably be expected to hold it.

During those times when you must be away from the home for several hours, it's time to introduce your Maltipoo puppy to an exercise pen.

Exercise pens are usually constructed of wire sections that you can put together in whatever shape you desire, and the pen needs to be large enough to hold your puppy's kennel in one half of the pen, while the other half will be lined with newspapers or pee pads.

Place your Maltipoo puppy's food and water dishes next to the kennel and leave the kennel door open, so they can wander in and out whenever they wish, to eat or drink or go to the papers if they need to relieve themselves.

Your puppy will be contained in a small area of your home while you are away and because they are already used to sleeping inside their kennel, they will not want to relieve themselves inside the area where they sleep. Therefore, your Maltipoo puppy will naturally go to the other half of the pen to relieve themselves on the newspapers or pee pads.

This method will help train your puppy to be quickly paper-trained when you have to be away for a few hours.

### e) Puppy Apartment™ Training

While a similar concept and a more costly alternative, the *Puppy Apartment*™ is a step up from the exercise pen training system that makes the process of crate or pen training even easier on both humans and puppies.

The Puppy Apartment™ works well in a variety of situations, whether you're at home and unable to pay close attention to your Maltipoo puppy's needs, whether you must be away from the home for a few hours or during the evening when everyone is asleep and you don't particularly want to get up at 3:00 a.m. to take your Maltipoo puppy out to go pee. The Puppy Apartment™ is an innovation that is convenient for both puppy and human alike.

What makes this system so effective is the dividing wall with a door leading to the other side, all inside the pen. One side of the Puppy Apartment™ is where the puppy's bed is located and the other side (through the doorway), is the bathroom area that is lined with pee pads.

With the bathroom right next door, your Maltipoo puppy or dog can relieve himself or herself whenever they wish, without the need to alert family members to let them out.

This one bedroom, one bathroom system, which is a combination of the kennel/training pen, is a great alternative for helping to eliminate the stress of worrying about always keeping a watchful eye on your puppy or getting up in the night to take them outside every few hours to help them avoid making mistakes.

According to *"Modern Puppies"*...

> *"The Puppy Apartment™ takes the MESSY out of paper training, the ODORS AND HASSLES out of artificial grass training, MISSING THE MARK out of potty pad training and HAVING TO HOLD IT out of crate training. House training a puppy has never been faster or easier!*
>
> *The Puppy Apartment™ has taken all the benefits of the most popular potty training methods and combined them into one magical device and potty training system. This device and system has revolutionized how modern puppies are potty trained!"*

Manufactured in the United States, this product ships directly from the California supplier (Modern Puppies).

The price of the Puppy Apartment™ begins at $138. USD (£83.37) and is only available online at Modern Puppies www.modernpuppies.com

## f) Free Training

If you would rather not confine your young Maltipoo puppy to one or two rooms in your home, and will be allowing them to freely roam about your home anywhere they wish during the day, this is considered free training.

When free house training your Maltipoo puppy, you will need to closely watch your puppy's activities all day long so that you can be aware of the *"signs"* that will indicate when they need to go outside to relieve themselves.

For instance, circling and sniffing is a sure sign that they are looking for a place to do their business.

Never get upset or scold a puppy for having an accident inside the home, because this will result in teaching your puppy to be afraid of you and to only relieve themselves in secret places or when you're not watching.

If you catch your Maltipoo puppy making a mistake, all that is necessary is for you to calmly say *"No"*, and quickly scoop them up and take them outside or to their indoor bathroom area. From your puppy's point of view, yelling or screaming when they make a potty mistake is unstable energy being displayed by the person who is supposed to be their leader and this type of behavior will only teach your puppy to fear and disrespect you.

The Maltipoo is not a difficult puppy to housebreak and they will generally do very well when you start them off with *"puppy pee pads"* that you will move closer and closer to the same door that you always use when taking them outside. This way they will quickly learn to associate going to this door when they need to relieve themselves.

When you pay close attention to your Maltipoo puppy's sleeping, eating, drinking and playing habits, you will quickly learn their

110

body language so that you are able to predict when they might need to relieve themselves.

Your Maltipoo puppy will always need to relieve themselves first thing in the morning, as soon as they wake up from a nap, approximately 20 minutes after they finish eating a meal, after they have finished a play session, and of course, before they go to bed at night.

It's important to have compassion during this house training time in your young Maltipoo's life so that their education will be as stress-free as possible.

It's also important to be vigilant because how well you pay attention will minimize the opportunities your puppy may have for making a bathroom mistake in the first place, and the fewer mistakes they make, the sooner your Maltipoo puppy will be house trained.

## g) Professional Cleaning Products

Remember that a dog's sense of smell is at least 2,000 times more sensitive that our human sense of smell.

As a result of your Maltipoo puppy's superior sense of smell, it will be very important to effectively remove all odors from house training accidents, because otherwise, your Maltipoo puppy will be attracted  by the smell to the place where they may have had a previous accident, and will want to do their business there again and again.

While there are many products that are supposed to remove odors and stains, many of these are not very effective. You want a professional grade cleaner that will not just mask one odor with another scent, but will completely neutralize odors.

**TIP**: go to www.removeUrineOdors.com and order yourself some *"SUN"* and/or *"Max Enzyme"* because these products contain professional-strength odor neutralizers and urine digesters that bind to and completely absorb odors on any type of surface.

## 2) Barking

Both malteses and poodles are known for being barkers, and this is a reputation that they have passed on to the maltipoo. One thing to remember is that even if a dog does not bark as a puppy, there is a chance that it will develop this behavior later on. It is not uncommon for a dog to be perfectly quiet until it is two or three years old and then to start to bark.

When your dog barks, it is important to determine why it is doing so. Maltipoos bark to communicate, and if you are misreading the message, you are not going to be able to make it stop!

Firstly, maltipoos will bark due to being alarmed. An unusual noise or something that is out of place to them can make them bark quite loudly.

Another reason that a maltipoo will bark is because of boredom. They are quite social little dogs, and when they are left alone for an extended period of time, they will quickly become lonely and bored. Barking is just one way that they blow off steam, and they can do it for a very long time and with a great deal of vigor.

If your dog is barking because it is lonely, this is something that you need to change in your own behavior. Dogs get lonely if they are left alone too long. If your dog is barking because you are away from home for hours and hours at a time, you need to have someone to come and check on your dog. Some dogs are fairly independent, but the maltipoo was bred to be a companion animal. They are known for bonding with people and requiring a lot of attention.

Remember that when your maltipoo barks, you should not react. For example, if your dog barks and you shout at it to be quiet, it does not necessarily understand that you are displeased. Dogs expect a call and response when they bark, so when you shout back, it is simply reinforcing the idea that there was something to be barking about in the first place.

Some dogs are naturally loud while others are inclined towards being quiet, but the truth is that they can all be trained to be quieter.

The next time your maltipoo starts barking, be patient. Wait until it stops, give a command like "quiet" or "hush," and wait for three to five seconds of quiet and then reward the dog with a treat or with a lot of praise. The timing on this exercise takes a little work, but the key is to show the dog that being quiet is rewarded.

You may also choose to distract your dog. When your dog starts to bark, make sure that you call the dog to you and ask it to do a favorite trick. If you are able to interrupt the dog from it's barking, you will find that it is less inclined to start.

Some dogs bark because they are uneasy or uncomfortable with something that happens or someone approaching. If your dog is having issues with strangers coming up the walk or with the postal worker showing up, you need to work on getting it more comfortable with strangers.

Bring your friends and relatives through your home and make sure that your dog stays calm when they come in. For example, you can allow a person into your home while keeping your dog close to you. When they start barking at the new person, soothe them and show them that the new person is not someone to be afraid of.

Some people wonder if anti-barking collars are a thing that should be used on their maltipoos. The American Society for the Prevention of Cruelty to Animals states plainly on their site that anti-barking collars are cruel, and on top of that, they are not effective.

An anti-barking collar simply uses a noise-sensitive device to detect when a dog is barking, and then releases an unpleasant stimulus to the dog. In some cases, it is an electric shock; in others, a spray of citronella mist. The issue with anti-barking collars is that they punish the dog for barking no matter why the dog is making the noise. These collars also simply train the dog not to bark when they have the collar on.

## 3) Play Biting

The maltipoo is one of the many small dog breeds that are often considered to be a bit nippy, and the truth is that this reputation owes a lot more to the owner than it does to anything related to the maltipoo itself.

All dogs nip when they are puppies. This is how they learn to use their muscles, and how they play with their littermates. As they get older, larger dogs are trained out of this behavior as it is considered more dangerous and more threatening. Too often, smaller dogs like maltipoos are perceived as non-threatening and this behavior is allowed to continue.

The truth is that a bite from a small dog can be just as dangerous as a bite from a large dog, and if your maltipoo ends up biting someone, it can result in a serious injury and even legal issues. Training a puppy to stop biting is something that can be quite simple. When your puppy chews on you or even takes your fingers in its mouth, simply say "No!" very sharply and very loudly. The ideal is to startle the puppy so that it lets go immediately. If that does not work, shake the puppy off and walk away. Ignore it for five to ten minutes. This sends the puppy the very clear message that playtime ends when it does this, and that biting is unacceptable behavior.

In many ways, you are simply enlarging on what the puppy's mother would do when the puppy is biting her too hard. She will bark loudly and walk away. Simply by imitating the puppy's mother, you will find that you can get results fast.

In general, it is a good idea to make sure that you do not roughhouse with your maltipoo. Not only is this dog rather small and delicate, especially as a puppy, you might be reinforcing issues that will be harder to train out as the dog gets older.

Restrict play to things like playing fetch, playing tug of war (but only with a single, specific toy), or simply walking around with your dog. Inviting a dog to play bite or to wrestle with you can confuse it as you are trying to teach it good manners.

## 4) Begging

Maltipoos are smart dogs, and even as puppies, they will know when some type of behavior gets them treats. This can result in a dog that eventually pesters people as they eat for food, and as is discussed in the chapter on feeding your maltipoo, human food should be avoided.

When you want to make sure that your maltipoo does not become a pest at family meals, make sure that you keep a few things in mind. Firstly, make it a point to eat before you feed your dog. Even if you and your maltipoo do not have identical mealtimes, at least allow your dog to see you eating. The person who eats first is the dominant person, so you are establishing your dominance in front of your dog.

When your dog begs at the table, ignore it or send it out. You should never enforce begging behavior by making an exception "just this once." As with all other aspects of training, be firm and be as consistent as you can.

Another thing to keep in mind is that your dog should only do tricks when you ask it to. If your dog comes up to you and shows off a trick that you taught it, ignore it or simply pet it the way that you normally would. Your maltipoo needs to remember that they get treats by doing things that you ask, not because they simply do something that they have learned.

## 5) Sit

Maltipoos are fast learners, and many people end up teaching their maltipoo puppies how to sit within a day. They still need to remind the dog of what to do for a little while, but on the whole, Malteses are obedient and eager to learn.

When you want your dog to sit, say the word "sit" and put a little bit of light pressure on the puppy's hindquarters. This is something that is very easy to do. Repeat the motion and the instructions for a while, and then see what happens if you say "sit" without pressing the puppy's hindquarters down. Most maltipoos are smart enough to pick up on this on their own!

## 6) Come

Maltipoos are quite clever, and they can learn their own names very quickly. Similarly, they can learn the command "come" quite quickly, especially if you have someone there to help you.

Start by having a person holding your maltipoo back. Walk across the room, and as you call to your dog, have the other person release them. Some people choose to reward the dog with a treat and gradually phase the treat out, while other people find that maltipoos are clever enough and attached enough to come without the food reward.

Make sure that they associate the command for "Come" with the motion of coming towards you. Repeat this exercise several times, working in five to ten minute increments. Remember that short sessions are much better for your dog than long ones are.

This is something that can greatly reduce the chance of your dog getting hurt. A dog that responds to your call can be verbally pulled away from harmful situations. While some dogs do have the urge to wander away and to stay with something that sounds interesting to them, most dogs can be taught to listen to your calls.

## 7) Heel

When a dog is taught to heel, it will learn to walk next to you when it is on a leash. It will not pull ahead of you, and it will not try to sit down and halt your progress. Heel is a very useful command, and when you take into account the fact that lunging on the leash can actually hurt your maltipoo's fragile throat, it becomes a very important skill.

Start by standing in one place with your maltipoo at your side on its leash and harness. Praise the dog or give it a treat when it stands still.

Take a few steps, saying heel and holding a treat in front of the dog. The dog will follow the treat, causing it to walk next to you. When the maltipoo has done this, reward it with a treat and lavish praise. Some dogs are very food oriented, and other dogs are more dependent on your praise. Simply work with your dog and see which side your maltipoo is on.

With every session, continue walking a little further and bringing the dog along with you. Over time, as the puppy gets used to walking by your side, phase out the treats and start simply rewarding the puppy verbally.

Eventually, most maltipoos will heel very quickly and easily. Remember when you are training a maltipoo puppy that you should keep your training sessions very short and sweet. End on a good note so that the maltipoo does not start to get upset or anxious when it sees the leash.

Many maltipoos can learn to heel without the leash, given enough training. This is something that is much more likely to happen when your maltipoo gets older, however. Excitable puppies often need the leash as a reminder to stay steady and to stay close to you.

Whenever you take your maltipoo on a walk, remember to make it heel. Most people train large dogs out of running off or lunging away because they can actually pull the leash out of your hands. While a maltipoo cannot do that, it is still dangerous to have the maltipoo lunging in different directions and possibly putting itself in harm's way.

A maltipoo that can walk quietly and calmly on its leash is one that is much safer for itself and the people around it. Crate training is a method that is used to help you keep your maltipoo calm and collected while you are away from home for short periods of time and to help the dog with house training. It capitalizes on the fact that your dog is drawn to small, cave like spaces, and that once it has established this spot as home, it will be happy there. Crate training is fairly simple, and many maltipoos take to it very naturally. It starts by purchasing a crate that is correctly sized for your maltipoo. If you get the dog a crate that is meant for its adult size, you may want to put a small plastic or cardboard box into the crate to make it feel more at home.

Let the dog get used to the crate on its own. Sit beside the crate and lure your puppy into it. Do not shut the door until you have done this a few times. Talk lovingly with your puppy and play with it. If you want to make the puppy even more comfortable, leave an article of your clothing with your scent on it in the crate.

Get your puppy comfortable with the crate, and start to lock it in the crate for a short amount of time. Stay with the dog when you do so. It is important that the dog gets a sense of security from the crate, which prevents it from associating the crate with social isolation. Do not be shocked or surprised if your dog yelps or cries for a little while. Do not let it out when it does so, or it will start to believe that the best way to get out of the crate is simply to make more noise.

Let the dog out when it has quieted down. Gradually, keep your dog in the crate for longer and longer periods of time. Once your dog can stand to be left alone in the crate for about thirty minutes, you can start to leave the room.

The reason why crate training works is because it creates a place that your dog considers its den. Dogs are naturally unwilling to relieve themselves where they sleep, and that means that they learn better bladder control as time goes on.

## 8) Separation Anxiety

Maltipoos are fantastic companion animals. They are very loving and very sweet, but the issue is that these traits can work against them sometimes. Because your maltipoo can bond so closely to you, you will discover that it can make it difficult for you to leave home for work.

Some maltipoos are fairly independent, but most will experience some stress when you leave the house. They worry that you will not come back, and they will feel very nervous and afraid. In many cases, this anxiety will manifest in undesirable behaviors. A maltipoo that is dealing with separation anxiety might chew on things and destroy them, bark, or urinate or defecate in fear and nervousness.

As a responsible owner, it is very important for you to treat your maltipoo's separation anxiety seriously and carefully. Remember that separation anxiety comes about because your dog loves you and does not want you to leave.

Get your maltipoo used to the idea of you leaving by doing a lot of rehearsals. Allow your dog to see you putting on your coat and getting ready to walk out the door. Walk out of the door, and then, before the maltipoo can start to cry, come right back. Greet the maltipoo calmly, and if it has some training, ask it to do a trick or obey a command. Then reward the dog.

As you practice this over and over again, extend the amount of time that you are gone until the maltipoo is comfortable with you leaving. As you can tell, this is something that is far easier to put into practice with a puppy than with a rescue dog. A rescue dog can benefit from this training regimen, but remember to take it more slowly.

When you leave the house for the day, there are a few things that you can do to make sure that your maltipoo puppy stays calm and secure. It seems counter-intuitive, but do not pet and hug your puppy a great deal before you walk out the door. This is something that feels right to humans, but for a puppy, it simply means that it will get a lot of love before being cut off abruptly.

Stop playing with your puppy a few minutes before you leave, and when you do walk out, do it without addressing the puppy at all.

Some people find that leaving a treat behind while they leave the house can calm their dog. Other people take it one step further and leave a container of treats behind. This container, usually a hollow tube with holes in it, is full of treats that the maltipoo can smell but not remove. Then, when you come home, give the puppy some treats from the tube, putting the tube away afterward until the next time you go to work.

Remember that maltipoos are highly dependent on you for love and comfort. If you can, think about coming home in the middle of the day to see your puppy. If you cannot, see if you can find someone else to do so. This can comfort your puppy a great deal.

More and more large cities are developing doggy day care programs. These programs allow you to drop your dog off to enjoy a lot of play and companionship while you are away. Your dog is cared for by trained staff, and it is will be introduced to other dogs in a safe and monitored environment.

Remember that your maltipoo is descended from wolves, meaning that they are pack animals. A maltipoo that is left on its own too much will be worried and fretful, and this in turn can lead to bad behavior and a lot of mental stress. Do what you can to make sure that your dog feels secure.

## 9) Socialization and Bonding

As small dogs, maltipoos are often accused of having Napoleon complexes or big dog complexes, where they do not seem aware of how small they really are. They may act aggressively towards large dogs or anything that they are not used to, and they might even attack things that are new to them.

This behavior is dangerous, and it can result in injury to your dog, another dog, or a person. Basically, it is a result of poor socialization, and it needs to be addressed in your dog's training.

Good socialization starts as soon as you bring your puppy home. Research has shown that dogs in general have a period between the ages of 3 weeks to 12 weeks when they are most malleable to new things. During this stage, they are curious and unafraid of the entire world, and they are very receptive. This period tapers off starting at 12 weeks, and by the time the puppy is 18 weeks old, it will be a little tougher to get it used to things.

If you are bringing your puppy home at the age of 8 weeks, that means that you have another month to two months to get your puppy used to the whole world and friendly with it. Puppies are much like children, and the more you expose them to at an early age, the happier and healthier they will be later on.

Among the things that you need to expose your puppy to are other dogs, other animals, people of all ages, children, people in uniforms, car trips, the veterinarian's office, crowds and vacuum cleaners. The list goes on, but in general, the more experiences that you can give your dog, the better.

One great way to start the process off is to take the dog to puppy kindergarten. These classes are often held at large pet stores or at shelters, and there you can get your dog used to other dogs and new people. Keep an eye on your puppy, and if it tries to bite or wrestle with the other dogs, say "no" in a loud and clear voice.

Puppy kindergarten might also guide your puppy through some basic commands, which you can then reinforce at home.

Even if your puppy is not strong enough yet for a long walk, you can still take it to the park. Sit at the park, and allow your puppy to get used to all of the people going by. If someone comes along who wants to pet your puppy, allow them to do so. This gets your puppy used to meeting new people and to handling from people who are not you.

Make sure that your puppy associates the car with fun and good times. If you only ever take your puppy to the veterinarian, you will find that it grows to be nervous and fretful around automobiles. Instead, if you make the destination the park, the house of a friend or something else enjoyable, getting your maltipoo into the car will be much simpler. While your maltipoo is small and can simply be picked up and carried to the car, it is far better to have a happy and curious dog in the back seat rather than one that is nervous and howling!

The more time you spend getting your puppy used to the world, the happier and more well adjusted it will be. Maltipoos have an advantage as they are very cute, small dogs, but this can cut both ways as they will go through their lives having people reach for them and pet them. People are not always good about asking permission, and it is far better to have them met by a dog that is unafraid and curious rather than fearful and snappish.

## Socializing within Different Environments

It can be a big mistake not to take the time to introduce your Maltipoo puppy to a wide variety of different environments because when they are not comfortable with different sights and sounds, this could cause them possible trauma later in their adult life.

Be creative and take your puppy everywhere you can imagine when they are young so that no matter where they travel, whether strolling a busy city sidewalk or along a deserted seashore, they will be comfortable.

Don't make the mistake of only taking your Maltipoo puppy into areas where you live and will always travel because they need to also be comfortable visiting areas you might not often visit, such as noisy construction sites or airports.

Your puppy needs to see all sorts of sights, sounds and situations so that they will not become fearful should they need to travel with you to any of these areas.

Your Maltipoo puppy will take its cues from you, which means that when you are calm and in control of every situation, they will learn to be the same.

For instance, put your puppy in their carrier bag and take them to the airport where they can watch people and hear planes landing and taking off, take them to a local park where they can see a baseball game, or take them to the local zoo or farm and let them get a close up look at horses, pigs and ducks.

When you take your Maltipoo puppy everywhere you will be teaching them to be a calm and well-balanced member of your family in every situation.

A good idea is to introduce your dog to new sounds by playing music of those sounds e.g. in a car or in the house and pretend everything is perfectly normal when the sounds are being played. If you do this when the dog is still very young, it is likely it won't care about "strange" noises.

A few examples of noises you could get your dog used to: airplanes, fireworks, the sound of a hoover, hot air balloon, crying children, a meowing cat, kids playing in the park, cars driving on the road, car hooters, a bicycle bell, thunder, etc.

There are CD's available online with all these sort of sounds recorded on for you to play in presence of your dog. Just search for it online.

## 10) Tips for Training Your Maltipoo

When you are looking to train your maltipoo, remember that you are dealing with a very clever puppy. Poodles are working dogs, and they are known to be very quick and very obedient. Malteses are known to be fairly bright, and although they are not as obedient as poodles are, they have excellent problem-solving skills. This means that you are definitely dealing with a puppy that has a mind of its own! Training a maltipoo puppy takes time and diligence, and you must always remember that the more training your maltipoo gets, the safer it will be. Train your maltipoo exactly the way that you would train a larger dog. Your maltipoo deserves the same level of consideration, and spoiling it as a puppy will only make it an unhappy dog that is difficult to deal with.

Remember that you should keep the training sessions simple at first. When your puppy is very young, even something as simple as wearing a harness or learning more about a toothbrush can be a little overwhelming.

Limit your training sessions to 10 minutes or less when your maltipoo is a very young puppy, and that means that it has a very short attention span. If you try to train your puppy for a longer period of time, you will likely discover that it's attention wanders and it will perform less successfully.

Determine how you will reward your puppy. While rewarding with treats is very handy, you should always phase it out as your puppy becomes more competent at the commands that you are trying to get it to carry out. Remember that dogs are very much people pleasers, and a puppy that looks up to you and loves you will be just as happy to perform because it pleases you.

Give your puppy plenty of playtime as well. Maltipoos are related to one working breed, the poodle, but the other side of its ancestry, the Maltese, is very much a companion animal. Maltipoos need to play as well as train, so block in plenty of time for just goofing around.

Never become angry or frustrated while training your maltipoo. Shouting or hitting your dog will only make it afraid and anxious, and in many cases, it will make your training take a longer period of time. It is far easier to make your maltipoo get the point if you ignore bad behavior, and reward good behavior.

When you catch your dog doing something that you do not want it to do, say "no" in a very loud and startling way. This can make the maltipoo puppy back off of the thing it was doing wrong very easily.

Unless you catch the maltipoo in an error, do not scold it. If you come home to find a pillow shredded to bits, you cannot scold the maltipoo unless you caught it in the act. If you scold when the maltipoo is not doing anything wrong, it will not make a connection between the issue and the scolding. Instead, this will simply make your dog very fearful.

When you are training your maltipoo, remember that the adage of rinse and repeat is a good one! The more reinforcement your puppy gets, the better, If you are tackling something difficult and your puppy looks frustrated or anxious, make sure that you stop and go back to another, easier lesson. This is a good way to end your lessons on a good note.

Remember that you are training your maltipoo to help it keep safe. Do not allow the training to get under your skin or to make you angry or frustrated. Be willing to be patient with your dog.

Good training is a lifetime commitment. There are people out there who think that they only ever have to train their maltipoos when they are puppies. The truth of the matter is that if you persistently train your maltipoo throughout its life, you are cementing your bond with the animal and you are making sure that it will listen to you.

A maltipoo is an extremely sweet and pleasant dog if you are willing to train it right. Do not think that being too yielding during training is a good thing.

## 11) Treats or Not?

Maltipoos, like any other dog, will happily eat every treat that you offer it.

When it comes to offering your dog treats, remember that you always want the treats to be a sign of your praise, not a simple thing that the puppy loves for its taste alone.

Some people choose to reward with praise alone and leave treats just as a bonding experience, while others reward primarily with treats. Choose an approach that feels good for you, but remember that your maltipoo loves to please you; in most cases, the treats won't even be necessary!

## a) Treats to Avoid

### Rawhide

Rawhide is soaked in an ash/lye solution to remove every particle of meat, fat and hair and then further soaked in bleach to remove remaining traces of the ash/lye solution. Now that the product is no longer food, it no longer has to comply with food regulations.

While the hide is still wet it is shaped into rawhide chews, and upon drying it shrinks to approximately 1/4 of its original size.

Furthermore, arsenic based products are often used as preservatives, and antibiotics and insecticides are added to kill bacteria that also fight against good bacteria in your dog's intestines.

The collagen fibers in the rawhide make it very tough and long lasting, which makes this chew a popular choice for humans to give to their dogs because it satisfies the dog's natural urge to chew while providing many hours of quiet entertainment.

Sadly, when a dog chews a rawhide treat, they ingest many harsh chemicals and when your dog swallows a piece of rawhide, that piece can swell up to four times its size inside your dog's stomach, which can cause anything from mild to severe gastric blockages that could become life threatening and require surgery.

### Pigs Ears

These treats are actually the ears of pigs, and while most dogs will eagerly devour them, they are extremely high in fat, which can cause stomach upsets, vomiting and diarrhea for many dogs.

Pigs ears are often processed and preserved with unhealthy chemicals that discerning dog guardians will not want to feed their dogs. While pig ears are generally not considered to be a healthy treat choice for any dog, they should be especially avoided for any dog that may be at risk of being overweight.

## Hoof Treats

Many humans give cow, horse and pig hooves to their dogs as treats because they consider them to be *"natural"*.

The truth is that after processing these *"treats"* they retain little, if any, of their *"natural"* qualities.

Hoof treats are processed with preservatives, including insecticides, lead, bleach, arsenic based products, and antibiotics to kill bacteria, that can also harm the good bacteria in your dog's intestines, and if all bacteria is not killed in these meat based products before feeding them to your dog, they could also suffer from Salmonella poisoning.

Hooves can also cause chipping or breaking of your dog's teeth as well as perforation or blockages in your dog's intestines.

## b) Healthy Treats

## Hard Treats

There are so many choices of hard or crunchy treats available that come in many varieties of shapes, sizes and flavors, that you may have a difficult time choosing. If your Maltipoo will eat them, hard treats will help to keep their teeth cleaner.

Whatever you do choose, read the labels and make sure that the ingredients are high quality and appropriately sized for your Maltipoo friend.

## Soft Treats

Soft, chewy treats are also available in a wide variety of flavors, shapes and sizes for all the different needs of our fur friends and are often used for training purposes as they have a stronger smell.

Often smaller dogs, such as the Maltipoo, prefer the soft, chewy treats to the hard crunchy ones.

## Dental Treats

Dental treats or chews are designed with the specific purpose of helping your Maltipoo to maintain healthy teeth and gums. They usually require intensive chewing and are often shaped with high ridges and bumps to exercise the jaw and massage gums while removing plaque build-up near the gum line.

## Freeze-Dried and Jerky Treats

Freeze-dried and jerky treats offer a tasty morsel most dogs find irresistible as they are usually made of simple, meaty ingredients, such as liver, poultry and seafood. These treats are usually lightweight and easy to carry around, which means they can also be great as training treats.

## Human Food Treats

You will want to be very careful when feeding human foods to dogs as treats, because many of our foods contain additives and ingredients that could be toxic and harmful.

Be certain to choose simple, fresh foods with minimal or no processing, such as lean meat, poultry or seafood, and even if your Maltipoo will eat anything put in front of them, be aware that many common human foods, such as grapes, raisins, onions and chocolate are poisonous to dogs.

**Training Treats**

While any sort of treat can be used as an extra incentive during training sessions, soft treats are often used for training purposes because of their stronger smell and smaller sizes.

Yes, we humans love to treat our dogs, whether to help to teach the new puppy to go pee outside, teaching the adolescent dog new commands, for trick training, for general good behavior, or for no reason at all other than that they just gave us the *"look"*.

Make sure the treats you choose are high quality, so that you can help to keep your Maltipoo both happy and healthy, and generally the treats you feed should not make up more than approximately 10% of their daily food intake.

## 12) Escapes

This breed is not known as an escape risk, but accidents happen, and before you know it, your dog might be lost on the streets.

Make sure that you put up notices throughout your neighborhood and that you are capable of getting word to the humane shelter, animal control and the local vets.

Go out looking for your maltipoo regularly, especially at dawn and dusk. Look close to buildings, underneath porches, and call the dog's name regularly.

Another thing that you can do is, if you get a tip stating that your dog has been found in a certain area, leave a shirt that you have worn for a day or two there. If you are lucky, your maltipoo will detect your scent on the shirt and stay there.

Remember that if your maltipoo does not come home right away, keep hoping. Sometimes dogs that disappear will show up again weeks or even months later!

# Chapter 8) Maltipoo Health

The maltipoo is a relatively new breed of dog, and as such, there is not a recognized list of maladies that are associated with them. However, there are still some conditions that crop up again and again in the maltipoo population and some conditions that they seem prone to due to their ancestry.

While there is no replacement for a good veterinarian, it is helpful to be aware of some of the issues that are faced by maltipoos and to be ready if they should occur.

There are some signs that tell you that your maltipoo is not well. For example, a change in temperament means that something is wrong, as does a change in attitude towards food. An ill maltipoo might also stagger as it walks or refuse to get up. You might notice it favoring one leg or having difficulty doing things that it could do before with ease.

Also remember that a dog that gags, looks like it cannot breath, or is shuddering is in a bad way. Look for excessive drool, eyes that roll back, or spasmodic twitching as well. Any of these signs are quite serious and require a veterinarian's intervention immediately.

Without a doubt, it is far better to be safe than sorry. Call the emergency veterinarian and ask them for further instructions. As new as the breed is, and as fragile as the dogs themselves are, maltipoos need all the help that they can get if they sicken.

If you are ever nervous about your maltipoo or feel that something could be serious, talk to your veterinarian right away. Maltipoos are small and relatively delicate, when they sicken, they can do so very quickly.

# 1) Tear staining

Tear staining is a condition that occurs in many dog breeds, but it seems very common in dogs with Maltese ancestry. This condition involves dampness from the dog's eyes staining the fur over time. This staining can also affect the fur around the dog's mouth, and in a very severe case, it can even affect the dog's paws. Tear staining leaves rusty reddish or brownish coloration around the affected areas, and there are several factors that might be at play.

Firstly, tear staining may be due to minerals in the water that your maltipoo is drinking. This is why many people who show Malteses professionally will only allow their dogs to drink distilled water or bottled water. The water can also become contaminated from the bowl. Stick with feeding and watering your dog from stainless steel containers for this reason.

There is also the chance that your dog has a minor yeast infection in these associated areas. Red yeast is a fairly harmless issue, but it can make your dog's appearance a little distressing. If you are concerned that this is what is affecting your dog, talk to your veterinarian for a round of antibiotics that can help. It is also worth noting that some veterinarians do not consider tear staining to be a serious issue. If the issue bothers you, however, find a veterinarian who is willing to help you solve it.

The best way to reduce tear staining is to reduce the tears themselves. Take a close look at your dog's eyes and make sure that none of its hair is pointing back towards the eye. Sometimes, the dog's fur grows in the wrong direction and irritates the sensitive tissue there.

There are several home solutions that you can use to get rid of tearstains that have already formed. For example, one common solution that works well on tearstains that are not so vivid involves creating a mix that is ½ lemon juice and ½ baking soda. Stir this mixture into a paste and apply it to your dog's tearstains. Then simply wait for five to ten minutes until the mixture is dry, and rinse it out. This is something that does require your dog to sit still, but it is quite effective.

Another home solution involves creating a mixture that is 1/3 milk of magnesia, 1/3 hydrogen peroxide and 1/3 cornstarch. This solution is one that can be left on overnight before being rinsed out.

In both situations, remember to rinse the paste out of your dog's fur thoroughly. Be especially careful with the lemon juice, which can irritate your maltipoo's sensitive skin!

After applying any kind of paste to your maltipoo's fur, you may discover that it is important to condition the fur afterwards. Both of these treatments dry out the hair a lot, and a bit of conditioner will keep it looking clean, soft and fluffy.

## 2) Anal Gland Issues

Maltipoos, like all dogs, have a pair of small, bean-shaped glands that rest directly underneath their anus. While the purpose of these genes is not known, the genes themselves are filled with a brown liquid that has a very pungent, quite unpleasant smell.

Most of the time, you will not even notice that your maltipoo has anal glands. They are relatively unobtrusive and difficult to see, even when you are bathing your dog. However, when your maltipoo's anal glands start having issues, there are a few very obvious signs.

Firstly, anal glands that are too full of liquid will cause your dog to scoot. This typically means that it rubs its rectum on the ground while dragging itself about by its forelegs. The dog may also be whimpering and crying as it does so. Issues with anal glands will also cause your dog to emit a strong, unpleasant odor.

If you notice either of these things, it is in your best interest to take action right away.

If you have a relatively strong stomach, you may be able to empty your dog's anal glands yourself. To do so, simply set your dog into the bathtub and, using two fingers, apply steady pressure to the protuberant anal glands. If something is wrong, the glands may be swollen to the size of large grapes. Press upwards and inwards until you see a dark fluid start to well up. Then take advantage of the fact that the dog is in the bathroom to bathe it quickly and easily!

If you cannot exert enough pressure to express your dog's anal glands, if you cannot find them, or if you do not think you can handle this chore, you can pass it on.

Most veterinarians will take care of your dog's anal glands for you, and they tend to be very practical about taking care of it. They can also tell you if there is some kind of blockage or infection there that might be worsening matters.

Another person who will take care of your dog's anal glands is the dog groomer. If you have your dog's fur professionally cared for, make sure that you ask the groomer to take care of this issue for you. This is a commonly offered service, and you will discover that it may cost a nominal fee or the dog groomer might be willing to do it free of charge.

## 3) Pattellar Luxation

Pateller luxation, also known as a luxating patella, is a common issue for small dog owners in general and maltipoo owners in particular.

Essentially, when a maltipoo has patellar luxation, it means that the dog's kneecap has slipped to one side. The kneecap, scientifically known as the patella, is a loose cap of bone that sits in the cradle formed by the femur and the tibia. Typically, the patella stays in the right place as the dog bends and flexes its leg.

When a dog has patellar luxation, however, the patella slips to one side or another, causing severe pain. Over time, as this happens more and more frequently, it can wear down the bony structures on the femur and the tibia that are keeping the patella in place. This leads to an increase in patellar luxation, and it can also result in arthritis in the joint after an extended period.

Some symptoms that your dog or puppy will suffer from include favoring one leg, soreness in one leg, pain that occurs when the dog has jumped down from something or swelling in the affected area.

One startling thing about this issue is that the dog only experiences pain when the patella is actually slipping to one side or the other. In most cases, particularly early on in the issue, the kneecap slips back into place almost immediately. One thing that often puzzles maltipoo owners is that their dog will suddenly yelp with pain, look very upset for a short time, and then continue as if nothing is happening.

If you see signs of this issue in your dog, speak to your veterinarian at once. There are four stages of patellar luxation, ranging from stage I to stage IV, and the earlier you catch it, the easier it is to treat.

Make a note of every symptom that your dog has, and make sure that you present them to the veterinarian. If the veterinarian does not have a lot of experience with small dogs, they may be willing to chalk the issues up to a sprain. While they may be right, it is always better to be safe than sorry, and that means X-rays.

When your maltipoo is suffering from a case of patellar luxation, you will find that treatment usually involves bed rest and the use of anti-inflammatory drugs. Keeping a maltipoo still and quiet can be a bit of a challenge, but you will find that it can be done. If you want to keep your maltipoo quiet, the best thing to do is to turn into a bit of a couch potato yourself. Stay with your dog, and keep it company. It will be much less inclined to roam if you are right there with it!

If your maltipoo's patellar luxation is serious, you will discover that the veterinarian likely wants to perform surgery to fix it. This is why it is so important to manage this issue before it becomes a problem. However, it is also important to remember that, in some cases, there is simply nothing that you can do. This is something that maltipoo crossbreeds are prone to, and it is considered an inheritable disease.

One way that you can spare yourself the heartbreak of patellar luxation is to make sure that you purchase your dog from a breeder who tests for this issue. This is a common issue that happens to many small dogs, and the tests are standardized for breeders that work with breeds like chihuahuas and Malteses.

Speak to your breeder about whether they have tested their sire and dam for the condition and also whether they have tested the puppies that they are selling.

## 4) Legg-Calvé-Perthes Disease

Legg-Calvé-Perthes Disease is a condition that is known to affect maltipoos, and it is something your breeder should test for. In this condition, the head of the femur, where it connects to the dog's hip, becomes degraded, and over time, it creates a weaker and more traumatized joint. This is a condition that shows up when your dog is between 5 and 8 months old, although there are some dogs that develop it later on when they are adults.

If you are worried that your dog might have Legg-Calvé-Perthes Disease, there are a few key signs to look out for. Watch for a gradual lameness that develops over about three months. The dog might start favoring the limb in question, and at a late stage, it might move with the leg completely off of the ground. The dog might whimper, cry or even snap when you touch the limb, or otherwise behave in a way that is strange. Dogs that were previously aloof might become extra friendly, and a sweet dog might even try to bite. When you feel the affected area, you may note that the muscles around the hip joint are very soft.

All of these signs mean that you should take your dog to the veterinarian. Legg-Calvé-Perthes Disease is an issue that can be diagnosed by X-rays, and if you tell your veterinarian about your suspicions, he or she should be able to give you the information that you need.

Treatment for Legg-Calvé-Perthes Disease depends on the situation. In some cases, the condition can be managed with cold applied to the area, anti-inflammatory drugs and plenty of rest. As time goes on, however, most veterinarians will recommend surgery to take care of the damaged bone and surrounding tissue.

This is a fairly major surgery for your dog, and afterwards, a fair amount of recovery and rehabilitation is necessary. After the surgery has been completed, it is essential that your dog stays very active, because otherwise the area will stiffen up as the surgery heals.

If you are concerned about buying a puppy that has this condition, talk to your breeder. This is a condition that should be tested for in all maltipoo puppies, and if there is even the slightest chance that your dog might have this issue, you will be informed.

## 5) White Dog Shaking Syndrome

White dog shaking syndrome is an issue that affects both Malteses and poodles, so it makes sense that maltipoos have this issue as well. Essentially this disorder causes body tremors that can range from fairly mild to completely incapacitating. The dog goes from behaving normally one moment to suddenly and violently convulsing.

This is considered a sudden onset condition, and a dog that has no history of the condition might suddenly begin to express it. The most common age to begin having this issue is between 1 and 2 years old, but there are cases of it starting earlier and later.

White Dog Shaking Syndrome is something that might be caused by a number of different issues. To rule out anything truly severe, the dog must undergo several tests at the veterinarian's office, where things like viral or bacterial infections can be ruled out. However, once the more dangerous effects are canceled out, you may simply be left with a diagnosis that says that this will happen to your dog from time to time.

Various treatments will be recommended to prevent the issue, the most common being steroids. If steroids produce a positive effect, your dog will simply end up taking a prescription on a regular basis, just the way a human with a similar issue would do.

If your dog is diagnosed with White Dog Shaking syndrome, you will find that your dog can still live a very full and happy life with you. The key is simply to identify the likely cause of the seizures and to reduce their prevalence in the dog's life.

For example, these episodes are often associated with stress or excitement. If your dog is one that becomes overexcited when new guests arrive, it might be best to crate it or to put it in another room when you have visitors. Do your best to reduce the stress that your dog needs to deal with.

Another thing that can cause tremors is exercise. Maltipoos have a ton of energy, and they love to work out, but unfortunately, their bodies cannot always take it. This means that you may need to take your maltipoo out for shorter walks.

Also make sure that you keep an eye on your dog when it is on the stairs. Dogs that are prone to these seizures can hurt themselves if they fall down the stairs during an episode. It may be a good idea to install baby gates at the top and the bottom of the stairs to keep your dog safe.

## 6) Tracheal Collapse

Tracheal collapse is a serious issue that affects maltipoos most frequently when they are very young. To understand this issue, it is important to understand the structure of a dog's throat. Essentially, a dog's throat is lined with rings of cartilage that hold it open. Sometimes, whether due to injury or congenital issues, the rings will start to collapse inwards, as though they were being squeezed. Tracheal collapse can occur for a number of reasons. Maltipoos that become obese can be prone to this issue, and maltipoos that lunge while collared and restrained can do this to themselves. This is why it is important to keep your dog's weight down and to make sure that while your maltipoo is a puppy and still has a very fragile throat that you simply use a harness and leash rather than a leash and a collar.

There are several signs that can tell you if your dog is experiencing tracheal collapse. Although this is a serious issue and although your dog will always need to be treated for it, your dog might also stagger on with this issue for quite some time before you notice. Listen for a honking cough or for the sound of choking. This is a sign that your dog is not able to get air into its lungs. On top of that, a dog that was formerly very energetic and active might want to simply lie down all the time as it cannot pull enough air into its lungs to work.

Check your dog's gums to make sure that they are healthy and pink. If you find that the gums are bluish in color, this means that you need to take it to the veterinarian immediately.

Depending on what is causing the tracheal collapse and how severe it is, there are a few different treatments that the veterinarian might offer. In the first place, the dog might be given different types of medication. Things like bronchial dilators, cough suppressants and anti-inflammatory drugs can reduce the issue, but if your dog does not heal, surgery will be required.

Assuming that the surgery goes well, there is a good chance that your dog will make a full recovery, without any lingering effects at all. For dogs that have had tracheal collapse because of obesity, the veterinarian will likely recommend a diet and an increased amount of exercise.

Remember that tracheal collapse is an issue that is considered to be quite serious for maltipoos, and that it should be treated right away. To prevent any throat damage to your puppy, make sure that you keep it on a harness rather than on a collar until it is fully grown.

## 7) Hypoglycemia

Hypoglycemia is a condition that refers to a sudden drop in blood sugar, and if it sounds familiar, that is because it affects humans as well as dogs. This condition can turn a happy, bouncy puppy into a listless and even comatose lump within a matter of hours, and it is important to know what you are dealing with.

Firstly, hypoglycemia is a serious problem for maltipoos as well as their two parent breeds. You are dealing with a very small, energetic dog, and these two characteristics together can make for some serious troubles before your dog learns moderation.

Essentially, a maltipoo puppy has tons of energy. It wants to run around all the time, getting its nose into all sorts of situations, and it is always very eager to spend all day playing. However, the issue is that because they are so small, they can carry less fuel than bigger dogs. They can wear themselves out very quickly, and this is where hypoglycemia comes in.

Not only can playing and lots of fun make them hypoglycemic, some rather sensitive maltipoos can become hypoglycemic due to stress. Stress burns calories and energy, and as a result, your puppy might end up feeling frail and shaky.

You must be aware of what hypoglycemia in small dogs looks like. In the early stages, your dog will appear to be suddenly weak or lethargic. It might stop playing and sit down. It might even look as if it is unaware of its surroundings or very distracted by small things.

In more severe cases, if the hyperglycemia is allowed to continue, your maltipoo will become unresponsive to you calling its name, and even if you are right in front of it, it might not really be able to recognize you. In the most severe cases, your puppy's feet or body will start to feel quite cool. This does sound quite alarming, but the key is to avoid panicking!

Because hypoglycemia is so common, it is a good idea to keep an eye on your puppy and watch out for any signs of weakness. The first sign to watch out for is a bit of listlessness or lethargy. When you see a bit of weakness, feed your puppy a small meal to see if it improves. This is the best course of action if your puppy is still responding to you.

If your puppy is not responding to you, there are a few things that you can do. Keep a high-calorie nutrition supplement in your home, and feed your puppy about 3 cc of it using a syringe. This is something that can make a huge difference right away. Many puppies that were feeling lethargic will perk right up. If the initial feeding works, continue feeding the puppy 6 more ccs of the supplement over the next 24 hours or so. Do not exceed 9 ccs of supplement.

The key is to get your maltipoo puppy eating again. If you try the supplement technique and the puppy does not respond immediately, it is time for you to take your puppy to the veterinarian. While hypoglycemia seems like a mild enough issue, remember that maltipoo puppies are quite fragile. A little bit of damage in the early stages can leave them feeling wobbly and unhappy for a long time.

There is never a good reason for a maltipoo puppy to be feeling tired and lethargic unless it has just worn itself out from healthy play. If you see signs of unnatural lethargy and a failure to respond, make sure that you take action at once.

## 8) Heat Stress

Maltipoos have inherited a certain amount of intolerance to heat from their Maltese parents, and because of this, they need to be cared for very carefully any time the weather spikes. When the temperatures hit about 80 degrees Fahrenheit, you will find that you need to keep a close eye on your maltipoo.

Maltipoos are like other animals in that they can regulate their own body heat to some extent, but after a certain point, their bodies want to shut down. They can go from being just fine to being in a seriously, dangerous condition in a very short amount of time.

When you are going through some hot time at your home, watch your maltipoo to see if it becomes very lethargic or if it starts panting a great deal. Panting is one way that dogs try to release heat, and if you see a lot of it, it is time to cool the dog down.

You might also see your dog stagger around, looking uncoordinated or confused. There might also be some discharge from your dog's nose, or you might see that its gums are turning a dark red.

Another thing to remember is that your maltipoo's temperature should be below 104 degrees Fahrenheit or 40 degrees Celsius when taken rectally. Anything above 104 degrees Fahrenheit or 40 degrees Celsius is cause for concern, especially if it does not go down readily. Anything that reaches 106 degrees Fahrenheit or 41.1 degrees Celsius is cause for an emergency veterinarian visit.

If you suspect that your dog has heat stress, you must take action immediately. Remove your maltipoo to a cooler area of the house and start using rags soaked in cool water to bring down its temperature. Do not use an ice pack or submerge your dog in cold water, as this can actually cause temperature fluctuations in the dog's body. Monitor your dog's body temperature, and when the dog's temperature drops, stop the cooling methods.

At this point, offer your dog some cool water to drink, but do not be surprised if it refuses. Heat stress is draining and your dog might not be up to taking liquid just yet.

If your dog does not recover completely with this treatment or if it continues to be frighteningly listless, go to the veterinarian.

When it comes to heat stress, preventing the problem is far better than curing it. Dogs that recover from heat stress can suffer from organ damage and require treatments that cut down their lifespan.

To prevent heat stress in your dog, simply start by being alert. High temperatures are always dangerous, and if your dog is having issues cooling down on its own, you need to step in. If the day outside is very warm, restrict play and outdoor activities. Simply bring your maltipoos inside.

No matter where your dog is going or hanging out, make sure that it has a water dish full of fresh, cool water in it available to it at all times. Heat stress is made far worse by dehydration.

Finally, never ever leave your maltipoo in the car by itself on a day that is going to get warm. The small amount of airflow offered by the windows is not enough to keep the dog cool, and even a mildly warm day can turn deadly hot for a dog trapped in a car. The glass allows heat in but traps it, turning the interior of your car into an oven. This is something that can seriously hurt your dog, so be mindful!

Some people choose to have their maltipoo shaved for the summer, but this is a poor idea. The dog's coat acts as an important protective layer between the dog and the sun, and maltipoos that have been shaved are even more at risk for sunburn because their skin is often so pale. A trim is one thing, but never have your maltipoo shaved to cope with the summer heat.

## 9) Poisoning

One of the best things about maltipoos is also a thing that can be very harmful to them. Maltipoos are wonderfully curious, and they always want to try new things. This can lead to serious issues where they end up ingesting something that they should not and becoming very sick because of it!

Household plants and cleaning products are at the top of the list of things that will harm your maltipoo if ingested, but there are some foods that you enjoy that can harm them as well. Chocolate is one such food, as is anything from the allium family, including garlic and onions.

Depending on the toxin that your dog has ingested, there will be signs that it is distressed. Make sure that you are aware of the signs that tell you that your dog may have been poisoned.

For example, gastrointestinal distress is a sign that your dog might be poisoned. These signs are quite easy to see, and they include vomiting, diarrhea and drooling. If your dog has ingested a relatively mild poison, it might refuse to eat or gag upon eating the food.

Some poisons can rupture your dog's stomach, causing bleeding. If you see that your dog is producing blood when it coughs, or you see blood in its urine or its stool, contact a veterinarian immediately.

Pay attention to your dog's feces and urine. If you see blood in the urine or if you see constant diarrhea, it is time to talk to the veterinarian. Maltipoos present a special challenge because it takes very little vomiting or diarrhea before they start becoming very dehydrated and vulnerable.

As soon as you can tell that your dog has been poisoned, call an emergency veterinarian as soon as you can. They will want to know all the information that you have, so tell them what you suspect your dog may have eaten. Depending on the situation, they may ask you to observe your maltipoo, or they might ask you to bring your dog in right away.

## 10) Choking

We do our best to make sure that our dogs only eat the things that we give them, but even the most diligent owner can miss something important. If your maltipoo is choking, it is important that you know what to do as soon as you see the issue.

Some signs that your dog is choking include a hacking cough, difficulty breathing, a lot of drool, or a hunched and pained posture. Look around for any bones or splintered toys that could have left debris in your dog's mouth.

First, carefully pull open your maltipoo's mouth. Look for anything that is lodged in the dog's mouth or throat. To do this, hold the maltipoo's snout firmly with one hand and use your free hand to pull its lower jaw down. Use your free index finger on the lower hand to sweep through the maltipoo's mouth for any debris or any obstructions at all.

If you can see an object in your dog's throat, use your forefinger to prod it until it is free.

It is easier to help a choking dog if there are two of you. Ask a friend to hold your maltipoo under one arm, holding its jaws open in the manner described above. Do not be surprised if the dog whimpers and squirms; it does not know that you are helping it. As your friend holds your maltipoo, try to find the obstruction and remove it.

Since your maltipoo is small, lift it in your arms and hold it upside down. Hold it close to your body with its tail pointing straight up. Hold the dog by wrapping your arms around its lower abdomen, keeping it securely in place.

As you do this, sway back and forth gently for twenty seconds. Stop, set the dog down and check its mouth again. The position and the swaying might have dislodged the object to the point where you can remove it.

If you cannot remove the object in your dog's throat at this point, and the dog seems to have no luck in dislodging it on its own, it is time to turn the matter over to the veterinarian.

Depending on the severity of the situation, the veterinarian might give the maltipoo a sedative to relax the throat and to make pulling out the offending object a little easier, or X-rays and surgery might be required.

To prevent choking, never give your maltipoo bones that might be shattered easily and clean up any small items that a curious maltipoo might put in its mouth.

# Chapter 9) A Quick Word About Breeding

When you have a maltipoo yourself, and when you know that your maltipoo is a very sweet-tempered and healthy animal, you may be tempted to consider breeding it. It makes a certain amount of sense, and there really is nothing that is quite as cute as very young maltipoo puppies.

However, the truth of the matter is that maltipoo breeding is best left to the professions. Getting a dog as small as maltipoos pregnant is always a rather dangerous endeavor, and on top of that, there is no way that you will be legitimately able to recoup the money that you spend on the puppies through the sales.

A single litter will not generate enough cash to pay for things like supplies and veterinarian services, which include checkups throughout the whole process and routine checkups on the puppies once they arrive.

Female maltipoos are very small and very delicate. There are many dog experts who believe that dogs should never actually be bred this small due to the issues that come with this small size. In the first place, they are very easily stressed, and the strain of carrying puppies for the length of the pregnancy can be dangerous.

A dog is pregnant for between 58 to 64 days, though smaller dogs like the maltipoo may end up giving birth faster. During this time, she will have issues eating, and in the end, she will be very slow and sluggish.

Depending on the maltipoo that you own, you may also find that she cannot deliver her puppies naturally, and instead must be given a cesarean section. Some breeders have had very small dams whelp naturally, while others find that biology is against them and they need to be given surgery to deliver their pups.

A cesarean section surgery is a pricey procedure, and if it needs to be performed, it can cost you upwards of 2000 dollars or 1200 pounds.

If this is your maltipoo's first pregnancy, you will absolutely want a veterinarian on hand when she goes into labor. A veterinarian can tell whether the dog's labor is progressing normally or if emergency care of some sort is required.

Pregnancy is dangerous for dogs as small as the maltipoo, and there is always the chance that you will lose your pet.

On top of that, you will find that because maltipoos are such a trendy dog breed right now, they do suffer from spikes and valleys in terms of popularity. One year, the puppies are all reserved before they are born, and the next, there is no one that is interested in adopting them. Breeding dogs, especially dogs that have as many potential issues as maltipoos, is something that is best left to people who are professional breeders. This is not something to undertake lightly, and in many cases, it simply contributes to the tragic number of dogs that end up in the shelters.

If you are thinking about breeding your maltipoo, speak to the breeder that you bought the dog from. Chances are good that they will tell you about the business and why you should not enter into it.

If you are still unconvinced, talk to your veterinarian. Most veterinarians have very strong opinions about dog breeding, and they can tell you what kind of problem it might be in your area.

The maltipoo crossbreed itself is still very, very new, and it is something that does not yet have much prestige in the professional dog-breeding world. It may never gain this prestige.

Be responsible and make sure that your dog is spayed or neutered. Not only will this ensure that your dog stays more content and more at ease, you will never have to worry about accidental mating at all.

Some people are interested in breeding first generation crosses, that is, breeding between a Maltese and a toy or miniature poodle. This will have many of the same issues that breeding a maltipoo with another maltipoo brings, and once again, you never quite know how to judge the market.

It is far better to leave dog breeding to the professionals and to make sure that your own maltipoo gets to spend its entire life comfortably and as a beloved pet.

# Chapter 10) Poisonous Foods & Plants

## 1. Poisonous Foods

While some dogs are smart enough not to want to eat foods that can harm or kill them, other canine companions will eat absolutely anything they can get their teeth into.

As conscientious guardians for our fur friends, it will always be our responsibility to make certain that when we share our homes with a dog, we never leave foods that could be toxic or lethal to them easily within their reach.

While there are many foods that can be toxic to a Maltipoo, the following, alphabetical list contains some of the more common foods that can seriously harm or even kill our dogs, including:

**Bread Dough**: if your dog eats bread dough, their body heat will cause the dough to rise inside the stomach. As the dough expands during the rising process, alcohol is produced.

Dogs who have eaten bread dough may experience stomach bloating, abdominal pain, vomiting, disorientation and depression. Because bread dough can rise to many times its size, eating only a small amount will cause a problem for any dog.

**Broccoli**: the toxic ingredient in broccoli is isothiocynate. While it may cause stomach upset, it probably won't be very harmful unless the amount eaten is more than 10% of the dog's total daily diet.

**Chocolate**: contains theobromine, a chemical that is toxic to dogs in large enough quantities. Chocolate also contains caffeine, which is found in coffee, tea, and certain soft drinks. Different types of chocolate contain different amounts of theobromine and caffeine.

For example, dark chocolate and baking chocolate or cocoa powder contain more of these compounds than milk chocolate does, therefore, a dog would need to eat more milk chocolate in order to become ill.

However, even a few ounces of chocolate can be enough to cause illness or death in a small dog like the Maltipoo, therefore, no amount or type of chocolate should be considered safe for a dog to eat.

Chocolate toxicity can cause vomiting, diarrhea, rapid or irregular heart rate, restlessness, muscle tremors, and seizures. Death can occur within 24 hours of eating.

During many holidays such as Christmas, New Year's, Valentine's, Easter and Halloween, chocolate is often more easily accessible to curious dogs, especially from children who are not so careful with where they keep their Halloween stash.

In some cases, people unwittingly poison their dogs by offering them chocolate as a treat or leaving a luscious chocolate frosted cake easily within licking distance when nobody is looking.

**Caffeine**: beverages containing caffeine (like soda, tea, coffee, chocolate) act as a stimulant and can accelerate your dog's heartbeat to a dangerous level. Dogs eating caffeine have been known to have seizures, some of which are fatal.

**Cooked Bones**: can be extremely hazardous for a dog because the bones become brittle when cooked, which causes them to splinter when the dog chews on them.

The splinters have sharp edges that have been known to become stuck in the teeth, and cause choking when caught in the throat or cause a rupture or puncture of the stomach lining or intestinal tract.

Cooked turkey and chicken legs, ham, pork chop and veal bones are especially dangerous. Symptoms of choking include:

- Pale or blue gums
- Gasping, open-mouthed breathing
- Pawing at the face
- Slow, shallow breathing
- Unconscious, with dilated pupils

**Grapes and Raisins**: can cause acute (sudden) kidney failure in dogs. While it is unknown what the toxic agent is in this fruit, clinical signs can occur within 24 hours of eating and include vomiting, diarrhea, and lethargy (tiredness).

Other signs of illness caused from eating grapes or raisins relate to the eventual shutdown of kidney functioning.

**Garlic and Onions**: contain chemicals that damage red blood cells by rupturing them so that they lose their ability to carry oxygen effectively, which leaves the dog short of oxygen, causing what is called *"hemolytic anemia"*.

Poisoning can occur with a single ingestion of large quantities of garlic or onions or with repeated meals containing small amounts.

Cooking does not reduce the potential toxicity of onions and garlic.

**NOTE**: fresh, cooked, and/or powdered garlic or onions are commonly found in baby food, which is sometimes given to dogs when they are sick, therefore, be certain to carefully read food labels before feeding it to your Maltipoo.

**Macadamia Nuts**: are commonly found in candies and chocolates. Although the mechanism of macadamia nut toxicity is not well understood, the clinical signs in dogs having eaten these nuts include depression, weakness, vomiting, tremors, joint pain, and pale gums.

Signs can occur within 12 hours after eating. In some cases, symptoms can resolve themselves without treatment within 24 to 48 hours, however, keeping a close eye on your Maltipoo will be strongly recommended.

**Mushrooms**: mushroom poisoning can be fatal if certain species of mushrooms are eaten.

The most commonly reported, severely toxic species of mushroom in the US is Amanita phalloides (Death Cap mushroom), which is also quite a common species found in most parts of Britain. Other Amanita species are also toxic.

This deadly mushroom is often found growing in grassy or wooded area near various deciduous and coniferous trees, which means that if you're out walking with your Maltipoo in the woods, they could easily find these mushrooms.

Eating them can cause severe liver disease and neurological disorders. If you suspect your dog has eaten these mushrooms, immediately take them to your veterinarian, as the recommended treatment is to induce vomiting and to give activated charcoal. Further treatment for liver disease may also be necessary.

**Pits and Seeds**: many seeds and pits found in a variety of fruits, including apples, apricots, cherries, pears and plums, contain cyanogenic glycosides that can cause cyanide poisoning in your Maltipoo.

The symptoms of cyanide poisoning usually occur within 15-20 minutes to a few hours after eating and symptoms can include initial excitement, followed by rapid respiration rate, salivation, voiding of urine and feces, vomiting, muscle spasm, staggering, and coma before death.

Dogs suffering from cyanide poisoning that live more than 2 hours after onset of symptoms will usually recover.

**Raw Salmon or Trout**: Salmon Poisoning Disease (SPD) can be a problem for anyone who feeds their dog a raw meat diet that includes raw salmon or trout. The cause is infection by a rickettsial organism called Neorickettsia helminthoeca.

Nanophyteus salmincola are found to infect some species of freshwater snails. The infected snail is eaten by the fish as part of the food chain. The dog is exposed to this only when it eats an infected fish.

A sudden onset of symptoms occurs 5-7 days after eating the infected fish. In the acute stages, gastrointestinal symptoms are quite similar to canine parvovirus.

SPD has a mortality rate of up to 90%, can be diagnosed with a fecal sample and is treatable if caught in time.

Prevention is simple, cook all fish before feeding it to your Maltipoo and immediately see your veterinarian if you suspect that your dog has eaten raw salmon or trout.

**Tobacco**: all forms of tobacco, including patches, nicotine gum and chewing tobacco can be fatal to dogs if eaten.

Signs of poisoning can appear within an hour and include hyperactivity, salivation, panting, vomiting and diarrhea. Advanced signs include muscle weakness, twitching, collapse, coma, increased heart rate and eventually cardiac arrest.

Never leave tobacco products within reach of your Maltipoo, and if you suspect your dog has eaten any of these, seek immediate veterinary help.

**Tomatoes**: contain atropine, which can cause dilated pupils, tremors and irregular heartbeat. The highest concentration of atropine is found in the leaves and stems of tomato plants, next is the unripe (green) tomatoes, followed by the ripe tomato.

**Xylitol**: is an artificial sweetener found in products such as gum, candy, mints, toothpaste, and mouthwash that is recognized by the National Animal Poison Control Center to be a risk to dogs.

Xylitol is harmful to dogs because it causes a sudden release of insulin in the body that leads to hypoglycemia (low blood sugar). Xylitol can also cause liver damage in dogs.

Within 30 minutes after eating a product containing xylitol, the dog may vomit, be lethargic (tired), and/or be uncoordinated. However, some signs of toxicity can also be delayed for hours or even for a few days. Xylitol toxicity in dogs can be fatal if left untreated.

Please be aware that the above list is just some of the more common foods that can be toxic or fatal to our furry friends and that there are other foods we should never be feeding our dogs.

If you have one of those dogs who will happily eat anything that looks or smells even slightly like food, be certain to keep these foods far away from your beloved Maltipoo and you'll help them to live a long and healthy life.

## 2. Poisonous Household Plants

Many common house plants are actually poisonous to our canine companions, and although many dogs will simply ignore house plants, some will attempt to eat anything, especially puppies who want to taste everything in their new world.

More than 700 plant species contain toxins that may harm or be fatal to puppies or dogs depending on the size of the puppy or dog and how much they may eat. It will be especially important to be aware of the more common household plants when you are sharing your home with a new puppy.

Below is a short list of the more common household plants, what they look like, the different names they are known by, and what symptoms would be apparent if your puppy or dog decides to eat them.

**Aloe Plant**: (medicine plant or Barbados aloe), is a very common succulent that is toxic to dogs. The toxic agent in this plant is Aloin.

The bitter yellow substance is found in most aloe species and may cause vomiting and/or reddish urine.

**Asparagus Fern**: (emerald feather, emerald fern, sprengeri fern, plumosa fern, lace fern) The toxic agent in this plant is sapogenin — a steroid found in a variety of plants. Berries of this plant cause vomiting, diarrhea and/or abdominal pain or skin inflammation from repeated exposure.

**Corn Plant**: (cornstalk plant, dracaena, dragon tree, ribbon plant) is toxic to dogs. Saponin is the offensive chemical compound found in this plant. If the plant is eaten, vomiting (with or without blood), loss of appetite, depression and/or increased salivation can occur.

155

**Cyclamen**: (Sowbread) is a pretty, flowering plant that, if eaten, can cause increased salivation, vomiting and diarrhea. If a dog eats a large amount of the plant's tubers, which are usually found below the soil at the root, heart rhythm abnormalities, seizures and even death can occur.

**Dieffenbachia**: (dumb cane, tropic snow, exotica) contains a chemical that is a poisonous deterrent to animals. If the plant is eaten, oral irritation can occur, especially on the tongue and lips. This irritation can lead to increased salivation, difficulty swallowing and vomiting.

**Elephant Ear**: (caladium, taro, pai, ape, cape, via, via sori, malanga) contains a chemical similar to that found in dieffenbachia, therefore, an dog's toxic reaction to elephant ear is similar: oral irritation, increased salivation, difficulty swallowing and vomiting.

**Heartleaf Philodendron**: (horsehead philodendron, cordatum, fiddle leaf, panda plant, split-leaf philodendron, fruit salad plant, red emerald, red princess, saddle leaf), is a common, easy-to-grow houseplant that contains a chemical irritating to the mouth, tongue and lips of dogs. An affected dog may also experience increased salivation, vomiting and difficulty swallowing.

**JadePlant**: (baby jade, dwarf rubber plant, jade tree, Chinese rubber plant, Japanese rubber plant, friendship tree). While the toxic property in this plant is unknown, eating it can cause depression, loss of coordination and, although more rare, slow heart rate.

**Lilies**: some plants of the lily family are toxic to dogs. The peace lily (also known as Mauna Loa) is toxic to dogs. Eating the peace lily or calla lily can cause irritation of the tongue and lips, increased salivation, difficulty swallowing and vomiting.

**Satin Pothos**: (silk pothos). If eaten by a dog, the plant may cause irritation to the mouth, lips and tongue, while the dog may also experience increased salivation, vomiting and/or difficulty swallowing.

The plants noted above are only a few of the more common household plants, and every conscientious Maltipoo guardian will want to educate themselves before bringing plants into the home that could be toxic to their canine companions.

## 3. Poison Proof Your Home

You can learn about many potentially toxic and poisonous sources both inside and outside your home by visiting the ASPCA Animal Poison Control Center website.

Always keep your veterinarian's emergency number in a place where you can quickly access it, as well as the Emergency Poison Control telephone number, in case you suspect that your dog may have been poisoned.

Knowing what to do if you suspect your dog may have been poisoned and being able to quickly contact the right people could save your Maltipoo's life.

If you keep toxic cleaning substances (including fertilizers and vehicle products) in your home or garage, always keep them behind closed doors. As well, keep any medications where your Maltipoo can never get to them, and seriously consider eliminating the use of any and all toxic products, for the health of both yourself and your best friend.

## 4. Garden Plants

Please note that there are also many outdoor plants that can be toxic or poisonous to your Maltipoo, therefore, always check what plants are growing in your garden and if any may be harmful, remove them or make certain that your Maltipoo puppy or adult dog cannot eat them.

Cornell University, Department of Animal Science lists many different categories of poisonous plants affecting dogs, including house plants, flower garden plants, vegetable garden plants, plants found in swamps or moist areas, plants found in fields, trees and shrubs, plants found in wooded areas, and ornamental plants.

# 5. Grass

Be aware that many puppies and adult dogs will eat grass, just because. Perhaps they are bored, or need a little fiber in their diet. Remember that canines are natural scavengers, always on the look out for something they can eat, and so long as the grass is healthy and has not been sprayed with toxic chemicals, this should not be a concern.

# 6. Animal Poison Control Centre

The ASPCA Animal Poison Control Center is staffed 24 hours a day, 365 days a year and is a valuable resource for learning about what plants are toxic and possibly poisonous to your dog.

**Poison Emergency USA**

**Call: 1 (888) 426-4435**
When calling the Poison Emergency number, a $65. US (£39.42) consultation fee may be applied to your credit card.

**Poison Emergency UK**

- Call Pet Poison Helpline 800-213-6680 (payable service)

- Call RSPCA 0300 1234 999

www.aspca.org = ASPCA Poison Control.

# Chapter 11) Caring for Aging Dogs

## 1. What to Be Aware Of

As a result of advances in veterinarian care, improvements in diet and nutrition and general knowledge concerning proper care of our canine companions, our dogs are able to enjoy longer, healthier lives, and as such, when caring for them we need to be aware of behavioral and physical changes that will affect our dogs as they approach old age.

A Maltipoo will be entering their senior years at around 8 to 10 years of age.

### a) Physiological Changes

As our beloved canine companions become senior dogs, they will be suffering from very similar, physical aging problems that affect us humans, such as pain, stiffness and arthritis, diminished or complete loss of hearing and sight and inability to control their bowels and bladder. Any of these problems will reduce a dog's willingness to want to exercise.

### b) Behavioral Changes

Furthermore, a senior Maltipoo may experience behavioral changes resulting from loss of hearing and sight, such as disorientation, fear or startle reactions and overall grumpiness from any number of physical problems that could be causing them pain whenever they move.

Just as research and science has improved our human quality of life in our senior years, the same is becoming true for our canine counterparts who are able to benefit from dietary supplements and pharmaceutical products to help them be as comfortable as possible in their advancing years.

Of course there will be some inconveniences associated with keeping a dog with advancing years around the home, however, your Maltipoo deserves no less than to spend their final days in your loving care after they have unconditionally given you their entire lives.

### c) Geriatric Dogs

Being aware of the changes that are likely occurring in a senior dog will help you to better care for them during their geriatric years.

For instance, most dogs will experience hearing loss and visual impairment. If a dog's hearing is compromised, then using more hand signals will be helpful.

Deaf dogs will still be able to hear louder noises and feel vibrations, therefore hand clapping, using a loud clicker or stomping your foot on the floor may be a way to get their attention.

If a senior dog loses their eyesight, most dogs will still be able to easily navigate their familiar surroundings, and you will only need to be extra watchful on their behalf when taking them to unfamiliar territory. If they still have their hearing, you will be able to assist your dog with verbal cues and commands.

Dogs that have lost both their hearing and their sight will need to be close to you so that they can relax and not feel nervous, and so that you can communicate by touching parts of their body.

Generally speaking, even when a dog becomes blind and/or deaf, their powerful sense of smell is still functioning, which means that they will be able to tell where you are and navigate their environment by using their nose.

### d) More Bathroom Breaks

Bathroom breaks may need to become more frequent in older dogs who may lose their ability to hold it for longer periods of time, so be prepared to be more watchful and to offer them opportunities to go outside more frequently during the day.

You may also want to place a pee pad near the door, in case they just can't hold it long enough, or if you have not already taught them to go the bathroom on an indoor potty patch, or pee pad, now may be the time for this alternative bathroom arrangement.

A dog who has been house trained for years will feel the shame and upset of not being able to hold it long enough to get to their regular bathroom location, so be kind and do whatever you need to do to help them not to have to feel bad about failing bowel or bladder control.

Our beloved canine companions may also begin to show signs of cognitive decline and changes in the way their brain functions, similar to what happens to humans suffering from Alzheimer's, where they start to wander about aimlessly, sometimes during the middle of the night. Make sure that, if this is happening with your Maltipoo at nighttime, they cannot accidentally harm themselves.

Being aware that an aging Maltipoo will be experiencing many symptoms that are similar to an aging human will help you to understand how best to keep them safe and as comfortable as possible during this golden age in their lives.

## 2. How to Make Them Comfortable

### a) Regular Checkups

During this time in your Maltipoo's life, when their immune systems become weakened and they may be experiencing pain, you will want to get into the habit of taking your senior Maltipoo for regular veterinarian checkups. Take them for a veterinarian checkup every six months so that early detection of any problems can quickly be attended to and solutions for helping to keep your aging Maltipoo comfortable can be provided.

### b) No Rough Play

An older Maltipoo will not have the same energy or willingness to play that they did when they were younger, therefore, do not allow younger children to rough house with an older dog. Explain to them that the dog is getting older and that as a result they must learn to be gentle and to leave the dog alone when it may want to rest or sleep.

### c) Mild Exercise

Dogs still love going for walks, even when they are getting older and slowing down. Although an older Maltipoo will generally have less energy, they still need to exercise and keep moving, and taking them out regularly for shorter walks will keep them healthier and happier long into old age.

## d) Best Quality Food

Everyone has heard the saying, *"you are what you eat"* and for a senior dog, what he or she eats is even more important as his or her digestive system may no longer be functioning at peak performance. Therefore, eating a high quality, protein-based food will be important for their continued health.

As well, if your older Maltipoo is overweight, you will want to help them shed excess pounds so that they will not be placing undue stress on their joints or heart, and the best way to do this is by feeding them smaller quantities of a higher quality food.

## e) Clean and Parasite Free

The last thing an aging Maltipoo should have to deal with is the misery of itching and scratching, so make sure that you continue to give them regular baths with the appropriate shampoos and conditioners to keep their coat and skin comfortable and free from parasites.

## f) Plenty of Water

Proper hydration is essential for helping to keep an older Maltipoo comfortable. Water is life giving for every creature, so make certain that your aging dog has easy access to plenty of clean, fresh water, which will help to improve their energy and digestion and also prevent dehydration, which can add to joint stiffness.

## g) Keeping Warm

Just as older humans feel the cold more, so do older dogs.
Keeping your senior Maltipoo warm will help to alleviate some of
the pain of their joint stiffness or arthritis. Make sure their bed or
kennel is not kept in a drafty location and perhaps consider a
heated bed for them.

Be aware that your aging Maltipoo will be more sensitive to
extremes in temperature, and it will be up to you to make sure that
they are comfortable at all times, which means not too hot and not
too cold.

## h) Indoor Clothing

We humans tend to wear warmer clothing as we get older, simply
because we have more difficulty maintaining a comfortable body
temperature, and the same will be true of our senior Maltipoo
companions.

Therefore, while you most likely already have a selection of
outdoor clothing appropriate to the climate in which you live, you
may not have considered keeping your Maltipoo warm while
inside the home. Now would be the time to consider doggy t-
shirts or sweater clothing options to help keep your aging
companion comfortably warm both inside and out.

## i) Steps or Stairs

If your Maltipoo is allowed to sleep on the human couch or chair,
but they are having difficulties getting up there as their joints are
becoming stiff and painful, consider buying them a set of foam
stairs so that they do not have to make the jump to their favorite
sleeping place.

### j) Comfortable Bed

While most dogs seem to be happy with sleeping on the floor, providing them with a padded, soft bed will greatly help to relieve sore spots and joint pain in older dogs.

If there is a draft in the home, it will generally be at floor level, therefore, a bed that is raised up off of the floor will be warmer for your senior Maltipoo, who will be much more comfortable sleeping in a cozy dog bed.

### k) More Love and Attention

Last, but not least, make sure that you give your senior Maltipoo lots of love and attention and never leave them alone for long periods of time.

When they are not feeling their best they will want to be with you all that much more because you are their guardian whom they trust and love beyond life itself.

## 3. What is Euthanasia?

Every veterinarian will have received special training to help provide all incurably ill, injured or aged pets that have come to the end of their natural lives with a humane and gentle death, through a process called *"euthanasia"*.

When the time comes, euthanasia, or putting a dog *"to sleep"*, will usually be a two-step process.

Firstly, the veterinarian will inject the dog with a sedative to make them sleepy, calm and comfortable.

Secondly, the veterinarian will inject a special drug that will peacefully stop their heart. These drugs work in such a way that the dog will not experience any awareness whatsoever that their life is ending. What they will experience is very much like what we humans experience when going under anesthesia during a surgical procedure.

Once the second stage drug has been injected, the entire process takes about 10 to 20 seconds, at which time the veterinarian will then check to make certain that the dog's heart has stopped.

There is no suffering with this process, which is a very gentle and humane way to end a dog's suffering and allow them to peacefully pass away.

# 4. When to Help a Dog Transition

The impending loss of a beloved dog is one of the most painfully difficult and emotionally devastating experiences a canine guardian will ever have to face.

For the sake of our faithful companions, because we do not want to prolong their suffering, we humans will have to do our best to look at our dog's situation practically, rather than emotionally, so that we can make the best decision for them.

They may be suffering from extreme old age and the inability to even walk outside to relieve themselves, and thus suffering the indignity of regularly soiling their sleeping area, or they may have been diagnosed with an incurable illness that is causing them much pain, or they may have been seriously injured.

Whatever the reason for a canine companion's suffering, it will be up to their human guardian to calmly guide the end-of-life experience so that any further discomfort and distress can be minimized.

## When There is Uncertainty

In circumstances where it is not entirely clear how much a dog is suffering, it will be helpful to pay close attention to your Maltipoo's behavior and keep a daily log or record so that you can know for certain how much of their day is difficult and painful for them, and how much is not.

When you keep a daily log it will be easier to decide if the dog's quality of life has become so poor that it makes better sense to offer them the gift of peacefully going to sleep or not. During this time of uncertainty, it will also be very important to discuss with a veterinarian what signs of suffering may be associated with the dog's particular disease or condition, so that you know what to look for.

Often a dog may still continue to eat or drink despite being distraught, having difficulty breathing, excessively panting, being disoriented or in a lot of pain, and as their caring guardians, we will have to weigh their love of eating against how much they are really suffering in all other aspects of their life.

Obviously, if a canine guardian can clearly see that their beloved companion is suffering throughout their days and nights, it will make sense to help humanely end their suffering by planning a euthanasia procedure.

We humans are often tempted to delay the inevitable moment of euthanasia because we love our dogs so much and cannot bear the anticipation of the intense grief we know will overwhelm us when we must say our final goodbyes to our beloved furry friend.

Unfortunately, we may regret that we allowed our dog to suffer too long, and find ourselves wishing that if only we humans had the same option, to peacefully let go, when we reach such a stage in our own lives.

# 5. Grieving a Lost Pet

Often we humans do not fully recognize the terrible grief involved in losing a beloved canine friend. There will be many who do not understand the close bond we humans can have with our dogs, which is often unlike any we have with our human counterparts.

Your friends may give you pitying looks and try to cheer you up, but if they have never experienced such a loss themselves, they may also secretly think you are making too much fuss over "just a dog".

For some of us humans, the loss of a beloved dog is so painful that they decide never to share their lives with another, because they cannot bear the thought of going through the pain of loss again.

Expect to feel terribly sad, tearful and yes, depressed because those who are close to their canine companions will feel their loss no less acutely than the loss of a human friend or life partner. The grieving process can take some time to recover from, and some of us never totally recover.

After the loss of a family dog, first you need to take care of yourself by making certain that you keep eating and getting regular sleep, even though you will feel an almost eerie sense of loneliness.

Losing a beloved dog is a shock to the system, which can also affect your concentration and your ability to find joy or want to participate in other activities that may be part of the rest of your life.

During this early grieving time, you will need to take extra care while driving or performing tasks that require your concentration as you may find yourself distracted.

If there are other dogs or pets in the home, they will also be grieving the loss of a companion, and may display this by acting depressed, being off their food or showing little interest in play or games. Therefore, you need to help guide your other pets through this grieving process by keeping them busy and interested, taking them for extra walks and spending more time with them.

Many people do not wait long enough before attempting to replace a lost pet and will immediately go to the local shelter and rescue a deserving dog. While this may help to distract you from your grieving process, this is not really fair to the new member of your family.

Bringing a new pet into a home that is depressed and grieving the loss of a long time canine member may create behavioral problems for the new dog who will be faced with learning all about their new home while also dealing with the unstable energy of the grieving family.

A better scenario would be to allow yourself the time to properly grieve by waiting a minimum of one month to allow yourself and your family to feel happier and more stable before deciding upon sharing your home with another dog.

The grieving process will be different for everyone and you will know when the time is right to consider sharing your home with another canine companion.

# 6. The Rainbow Bridge Poem

*"Just this side of heaven*
*is a place called Rainbow Bridge.*

*When an animal dies that has been*
*especially close to someone here,*
*that pet goes to Rainbow Bridge.*
*There are meadows and hills for all of our special friends*
*so they can run and play together.*
*There is plenty of food, water and sunshine,*
*and our friends are warm and comfortable.*

*All the animals who had been ill and old*
*are restored to health and vigor;*
*those who were hurt or maimed*
*are made whole and strong again,*
*just as we remember them in our dreams*
*of days and times gone by.*
*The animals are happy and content,*
*except for one small thing;*
*they each miss someone very special to them,*
*who had to be left behind.*

*They all run and play together,*
*but the day comes when one suddenly stops*
*and looks into the distance.*
*His bright eyes are intent; His eager body quivers.*
*Suddenly he begins to run from the group,*
*flying over the green grass,*
*his legs carrying him faster and faster.*

*You have been spotted,*
*and when you and your special friend finally meet,*
*you cling together in joyous reunion,*
*never to be parted again.*
*The happy kisses rain upon your face;*

173

*your hands again caress the beloved head,*
*and you look once more into the trusting eyes*
*of your pet, so long gone from your life*
*but never absent from your heart.*

*Then you cross Rainbow Bridge together...."*

- Author unknown

## 7. Memorials

There are as many unique ways to honor the passing of a beloved pet, as each of our furry friends is unique and special to us.

For instance, you may wish to have your furry friend cremated and preserve their ashes in a special urn or sprinkle their ashes along their favorite walk.

Perhaps you will want to have a special marker, photo bereavement, photo engraved Rainbow Bridge Poem, or wooden plaque created in honor of your lost friend.

You may wish to keep their memory close to you at all times by having a DNA remembrance pendant or bracelet designed.

There are support groups, such as Rainbow Bridge, which is a grief support community, to help you and your family through this painful period of loss and grief.

# Maltipoo Resources

## 1) Information

http://www.designercanineregistry.com

The International Designer Canine Registry is one of the older registries for designer breeds from all over the world.

## 2) Breeders

http://club.net/html/breeds/maltepoo.htm

A unmoderated list of maltipoo breeders in the United States. At the moment, there does not seem to be a comparable list in the UK.

### 3) Food

http://www.nutro.com/natural-pet-food.aspx?sc_cid=paidsearch

Natural dog food with no grain. This producer has a small breeds brand that is great for maltipoos.

http://www.naturalbalanceinc.com/

Highly recommended by many maltipoo owners.

http://www.naturesmenu.co.uk/

Well-reviewed dog food from the UK.

http://burnspet.co.uk/

UK dog food manufacturer with excellent reviews.

## 4) Equipment

http://www.smalldogmall.com/store/

Fun and fashionable accessories, including well sized collars and leashes.

http://www.gollygear.com/

All items designed for small dogs.

http://www.petplanet.co.uk/

Wide range of small dog supplies from the UK.

http://www.petcrazy.co.uk/

Many pet supplies with a good selection of items for small dogs.

# Index

| | |
|---|---|
| adult | 10, 30, 60, 63, 69, 103, 118 |
| aggression | 15, 30, 71 |
| agility | 28 |
| American Kennel Club | 12, 28 |
| anal glands | 79, 132, 133 |
| antifreeze | 39 |
| anus | 132 |
| apartment | 31 |
| baby gates | 44, 137 |
| Baby gates | 39 |
| bark | 31, 35, 64, 112, 113, 114, 119 |
| Bark | 112 |
| bath | 62, 76, 77, 78, 84, 132, 133 |
| Bath | 77 |
| bed | 44, 54, 70, 134 |
| beg | 12, 14, 115, 136 |
| bladder | 16, 118 |
| bleaching solutions | 92 |
| booties | 62 |
| breeder | 13, 22, 23, 25, 26, 27, 29, 34, 44, 57, 135, 136, 146 |
| Breeder | 25 |
| breeding | 13, 22, 23, 25, 26, 64, 145, 146, 147 |
| Breeding | 145 |
| brush | 57, 75, 84, 88, 89 |
| car | 38, 58, 121, 141 |
| carriers | 15 |
| cats | 23, 31, 35, 62 |
| Cats | 35 |
| cesarean section | 145 |
| chewing | 39, 63, 89 |
| Chewing | 63 |
| children | 31, 32, 43, 121 |
| Children | 43 |
| choking | 15, 56, 138, 143, 144 |
| cold | 62, 77, 78, 135, 141 |

| | |
|---|---|
| Cold | 63 |
| collar | 15, 54, 55, 72, 113, 114, 137, 138 |
| color | 11, 81, 92, 138 |
| comb | 57, 75, 78 |
| cornstarch | 57, 81, 132 |
| crate | 58, 59, 70, 118, 137 |
| crossbreeds | 14, 134 |
| dam | 25, 27, 135 |
| dander | 13, 14 |
| ears | 76 |
| electrical cords | 39 |
| energy | 11, 12, 28, 30, 31, 61, 137, 139 |
| exercise | 12, 24, 61, 62, 113, 116, 137, 138 |
| eyes | 14, 131 |
| families | 9 |
| family | 9, 27, 30, 31, 115, 142 |
| fear | 15, 30, 70, 71, 119 |
| feeding | 60, 61, 115, 131, 140 |
| food | 44, 54, 55, 59, 60, 61, 70, 115, 116, 117, 142, 175 |
| Food | 55 |
| genetic | 13, 28, 29, 75 |
| grain | 175 |
| groomer | 78, 79, 81, 84, 89, 133 |
| grooming | 29, 57, 73, 75, 78, 79, 84 |
| Grooming | 73, 78 |
| harness | 55, 117, 124, 137, 138 |
| Harness | 54, 55 |
| heat stress | 141 |
| Heat stress | 141 |
| heel | 116 |
| hybrid | 9, 28, 29 |
| Hybrid | 28 |
| hypoallergenic | 13, 14 |
| hypoglycemia | 138, 139, 140 |
| insurance | 34 |
| Insurance | 34 |
| leash | 15, 55, 64, 116, 117, 137 |
| Legg-Calvé-Perthes | 135 |

| | |
|---|---|
| Legg-Calvé-Perthes | 135 |
| Legg-Calvé-Perthes | 135 |
| Legg-Calvé-Perthes | 135 |
| lethargy | 139, 140 |
| litter | 26, 27, 114, 145 |
| Maltese | 11, 12, 13, 14, 22, 29, 57, 60, 75, 78, 83, 84, 124, 131, 146 |
| mat | 75, 76, 78, 84 |
| microchip | 72 |
| Napoleon complexes | 120 |
| neutering | 64, 65 |
| North American Maltipoo Club and Registry | 12 |
| nutrition | 25, 55, 139 |
| obedience | 12, 28, 29 |
| other dog | 12, 13, 34, 35, 61, 64, 71, 84, 117, 120, 121 |
| Other Dog | 34 |
| park | 92, 121 |
| pet shop | 24 |
| Pet Shop | 24 |
| plants | 39, 142 |
| poodle | 10, 12, 13, 14, 22, 29, 57, 60, 83, 84, 124, 146 |
| Poodle | 78 |
| prey | 35 |
| puppy room | 45 |
| purse | 14, 15, 16 |
| Purse | 14 |
| rescue | 24, 25, 44, 69, 70, 71, 72, 87, 119 |
| Rescue | 69 |
| shaking | 136 |
| Shaking | 136, 137 |
| shampoo | 77, 78, 92 |
| shelter | 30 |
| sire | 25, 135 |
| sit | 116 |
| spaying | 64 |
| Spaying | 64 |
| stairs | 38, 39, 137 |
| superb companion animal | 10 |

tearstaining                                                                   131
teeth                                               57, 63, 87, 88, 89
temperament                                            12, 25, 102
toenails                                                         79, 80
toothbrushing                                                   63, 87
towel                                              44, 54, 58, 59, 78
toy              10, 12, 43, 44, 56, 59, 62, 63, 115, 143, 146
tracheal collapse                                            137, 138
training           12, 62, 115, 117, 118, 119, 120, 123, 124, 125
Training                                                            123
veterinarian    42, 43, 55, 58, 60, 61, 64, 72, 76, 89, 121, 130, 131,
133, 134, 135, 136, 138, 140, 141, 142, 143, 144, 145, 146
yeast infection                                                     131

## Published by IMB Publishing 2014

CPSIA information can be obtained at www.ICGtesting.com
Printed in the USA
LVOW04s0018260515

439765LV00017B/227/P